Edited Book

ADVANCES IN PHARMACEUTICAL SCIENCES

Editors

Dr. P. Saranraj
Department of Microbiology, Sacred Heart College (Autonomous), Tirupattur - 635 601, Tamil Nadu, India.

Dr. Padmaja Santosh Kore
Department *of Pharmacology, Progressive Education Society's Modern* College of Pharmacy, Yamunanagar, Nigdi, Pune, Maharashtra, India

Dr. Narayan Dattatraya Totewad
Department of Microbiology, B. K. Birla College of Arts, Science and Commerce (Autonomous), Kalyan West, Kalyan - 421 304, Thane, Maharashtra, India.

Published by

JPS Scientific Publications
India

Published by

JPS Scientific Publications, Tamil Nadu, India.
E.mail: jpsscientificpublications@gmail.com
Website: www.jpsscientificpublications.com

Published in India.

International Standard Book Number (ISBN): 978-81-951323-7-9

JPS Scientific Publications also publishes its books in a variety of Electronic formats. Some content that appears in print may not be available in Electronic formats. For more information visit our publication website www.jpsscientificpublications.com

ISBN: 978-81-951323-7-9

ABOUT THE EDITOR – Dr. P. Saranraj

Dr. P. Saranraj is presently an Assistant Professor and Head at the Department of Microbiology, Sacred Heart College (Autonomous), Tirupattur, Tamil Nadu, India. Prior to this he has worked as a Senior Research Fellow in Department of Microbiology, Annamalai University for 3 years. He is having teaching experience of 7 years and he has guided 10 M.Sc students for their project. He has been involved with teaching and research in area of Microbiology and Biochemistry. He received his Ph.D Microbiology degree from Annamalai University in 2013 and he was qualified in NET exam in 2017. He has published 167 papers (Citations – 2821, H - index: 30 and i10 index - 70) in peer reviewed International Journals, 56 Books and 20 Book chapters. He is an Editorial Board Member and Reviewer of 30 International Journals. He has also involved himself in filing an International Innovation Patent granted by the Government of Australia (AusPat) and Six Innovation Patents were Granted. He has deposited 6 Bacterial Sequence in NCBI and received the Accession Number. He was also conferred with awards like Best Review Paper Award (2011), Young Scientist Award (2013), Best Research Forum Coordinator Award (2017), Highest Book Publication Award (2017), Best Review Paper Award (2017), Highest Research Paper Publication Award (2018), Young Researcher Award (2018), Best Research Forum Coordinator Award (2019), Indian Microbiologists Society Young Scientist Award (2019), Highest Citations Award (2019), Best Research Forum Coordinator Award (2020), Research Excellence Award (2020), Young Academic Achiever Award (2020) and Microbiology Young Scientist Award (2021). According to AD Scientific Index World Scientist Ranking (Microbiology), his name was placed in 34th Rank in India Level, 131th Rank in Asia Level and 570th Rank in World. He is a life member in various organizations viz., Microbiologists Association, India and Asian PGPR Society.

ABOUT THE EDITOR – Dr. Padmaja Santosh Kore

Dr. Padmaja Santosh Kore is working as Assistant Professor at the Department of Pharmacology, Progressive Education Society's Modern College of Pharmacy, Yamunanagar, Nigdi, Pune - 44 since 2017 till date. Prior to this, she was associated with MAEER's Maharashtra Institute of Pharmacy since 2011. She is having teaching experience of 12 years and she has guided 2 M-Pharm students for their project. She has published various review and research papers in peer reviewed national and international research journals. She was awarded with best oral research paper award by ICSCCB-2015 organized at Pune. She has presented oral research papers in some international conferences. She has reviewed 4 research papers and published several book chapters in national books and also there are 5 upcoming book chapters in international books.

ABOUT THE EDITOR – Dr. Narayan Dattatraya Totewad

Dr. Narayan Dattatraya Totewad is currently working as Assistant Professor in Microbiology at B. K. Birla College of Arts, Science & Commerce (Autonomous), Kalyan, Dist. Thane, Maharashtra. He has 7 years of Teaching and 14 years of Research Experience. He completed his graduation from N. E. S. Science College, Nanded, post-graduation in Microbiology and awarded Ph.D. in Biotechnology on topic "Probiotics as feed supplement for growth and development of potential aquatic organisms under the guidance of Dr. G. Gyananath on 13th July 2013, School of Life Sciences, Swami Ramanand Teerth Marathwada University, Nanded, Maharashtra. He awarded with UGC- Rajiv Gandhi National Junior and Senior Research Fellowship (2007 to 2012) to pursue Ph.D. degree. He also completed post-graduate diploma with distinction in Bio-nanotechnology in the year 2020 from B. K. Birla College (Autonomous), Kalyan. His area of research interest is Basic and Applied Microbiology, Bio-nanotechnology, Environmental Science, Food Microbiology and Biomedical Sciences. He has deposited four bacterial sequences to NCBI and received the accession number. Three Australian Innovation Patents granted, and five Indian Patents published in Indian Patent Journal, India. He has published 12 papers in National and International Journals of well repute. He published 2 books, edited 4 books and written 7 book chapters in various science books. In the year 2021, he was honoured with Excellence and Innovation Award in Microbiology for the year 2020, from Pearl- A Foundation for Educational Excellence Awards to Higher Education in India. He was selected as Mentor by CSIR-Summer Research Training Programme-2020 conducted by CSIR Jorhat, Assam, India and Guided 11 students across India.

Contents

Advances in Pharmaceutical Sciences
ISBN: 978-81-951323-7-9
First Edition; Volume – 1; 2021
Chapter – 1, Page: 1 - 10

1

PHYTATE: A BOON TO PHARMACEUTICALS

Suchita Bharambe[1] and Swati Peshwe[2]

[1]Department of Microbiology, Government College of Arts and Science, Aurangabad, Maharashtra, India

[2]Department of Microbiology, Government Institute of Science, Aurangabad, Maharashtra, India

*Corresponding author: suchitabharambe@gmail.com

Abstract

Phytate/Phytic acid [myo-inositol(1,2,3,4,5,6)hexakisphosphate] is the main storage form of Phosphorus (P) in many plants. Numerous physiological roles have been suggested for phytic acid in seeds and grains *viz.*, phosphorus store, energy store, source of cations, source of myo-inositol (a cell wall precursor), and initiation of dormancy. However, the phytic acid exhibits antinutrients action by chelating the positively charged multivalent cations, proteins and amino acids in foods thereby reducing the energy uptake. Phytic acid also have significance in human nutrition and food and feed technology. In addition, it has therapeutic significance. This review discuses about therapeutic potential of phytic aid as anticancer, antidiabetics, anti-inflammatory, antiplatelet and antihyperlipidemic.

Key words: Phytate, Antinutrient, Therapeutic significance, Anticancer and Antioxidant.

1. Introduction

Phytic acid [*myo*-inositol(1,2,3,4,5,6)hexakisphosphate/IP6] is the main storage form of phosphorus (P) in many plants. Cereals, leguminous and oil seeds plant contain 1 – 5 % Phytic acid which contribute about 50 – 80 % of total phosphorous present in seeds used in food/feed. This phytate phosphorous from plant sources is poorly digested and cannot meet nutritional requirement of animals specially in case of monogastric animals who lack the phytic acid hydrolysing enzyme *myo*-inositol hexakisphosphate phosphohydrolase [Phytase]. Phytase catalyses stepwise removal inorganic phosphate from phytic acid. Hence such unhydrolyzed phytic acid is excreted out in the environment which leads to eutrophication like environmental issue. Additionally, the phytic acid shows antinutritive effect in animals owing to its ability to form a chelate with divalent mineral ions *viz.*, Ca, Zn (Manary *et al.*, 2002). Phytic acid also binds to amino acids and proteins, inhibits digestive enzymes (Pallauf and Rimbach, 1996). However, Harland and Morris (1995) reviewed the presence of phytate in human diets is also claimed to have potential benefits, including anti-carcinogenic properties. Feil (2001) reported importance of phytate in human nutrition, medical science, food and feed technology, plant physiology and plant breeding. Phytases also have an important contribution in controlling diabetes mellitus, atherosclerosis, coronary heart disease and ceasing of stone formation in kidneys, inhibition of human immunodeficiency virus (HIV) and heavy metal toxicities.

Phytic acid is the major storage form of phosphorus in cereals, legumes and oilseeds. The systematic name of phytic acid is myo-inositol 1,2,3,4,5,6-hexakis dihydrogen phosphate (IUPAC-IUB, 1977). However, the term phytate, refers to the mixed salt of phytic acid and the term phytin, specifically refers to the deposited complex of phytic acid with potassium, magnesium and calcium as it occurs in plants, whereas phytic acid is the free form of IP6. The aleurone layer is the major site of phytate deposition in most cereals, whereas it is distributed uniformly throughout the kernels in dicotyledonous seeds, including oilseeds and grain legumes (Lott, 1984). In cereals and legumes phytic acid accumulates in the aleurone particles and globoid crystals, respectively (Reddy *et al.*, 1989). Endosperm of wheat and rice kernels is almost devoid of phytate, as it concentrates in the germ and aleurone layers of the cells of the kernel. Phytin function as sources of phosphate, myo-inositol and cations during seed germination (Reddy *et al.*, 1982). Several physiological roles have been suggested for phytic acid in seeds and grains *viz.,* phosphorus store, energy store, source of cations, source of myo-inositol (a cell wall precursor), and initiation of dormancy. In addition, phytic acid probably serves several other unknown functions in seeds (Reddy *et al.*,1989). Phytic acid shows an antineoplastic effect in animal models of both colon and breast carcinomas. The presence of undigested phytic acid in the colon may protect against the development of colonic carcinoma (Dvorakova, 1998). In seeds dormancy phytic acid have a natural antioxidant property based on the assumption that phytic acid effectively blocks iron-driven hydroxyl radical formation.

2. Phytic acid as Anti-inflammatory agent

Phytic acid (IP6) show anti-inflammatory activity, it was reported in liver tissue of iron overload induced liver injury in mice that IP6 reduced hepatocellular necrosis, proinflammatory cytokines mRNA including tumor necrosis factor alpha, interleukin 6 and interleukin I-beta (Bhowmik *et al.,* 2017). Graf (1985) conveyed that phytic acid rich diet suppress the inflammatory bowel disease. On account of its capacity to suppress inflammation and release of cytokines IP6 and myoinositols has valuable efficacy for Sars-Cov-2 patients (Bizzarri, 2020).

3. Phytic acid as Anticarcinogen

Various *in vitro* studies reveal the antiproliferative proficiency phytic acid against numerous cancer cells *viz.*, human leukemic hematopoietic cell lines k-562, human colon cancer cells-HT-29, breast cancer cells, prostate cancer, pancreatic cancer. The deregulation of myo-inositol and IP6 metabolism results in cancer where inositol modifies different critical pathways. Inositols inhibit pRB phosphorylation, fostering the pRB/E2F complexes formation and blocking progression along the cell cycle. Inositols reduce PI3K levels, thus counteracting the activation of the PKC/RAS/ERK pathway downstream of PI3K activation. Upstream of that pathway, inositols disrupt the ligand interaction between FGF and its receptor as well as with the EGF-transduction processes involving IGF-II receptor and AP-1 complexes. Additionally, Akt activation is severely impaired upon inositol addition. Downregulation of both Akt and ERK leads consequently to NF-kB inhibition and reduced expression of inflammatory markers (COX-2 and PGE2). Remarkably, inositol-induced downregulation of presenilin-1 interferes with the epithelial mesenchymal transition and reduces Wnt-activation, β-catenin translocation, Notch-1, N-cadherin, and SNAI1 release. Inositols interfere also with the cytoskeleton by upregulating Focal Adhesion Kinase and E-cadherin and decreasing Fascin and Cofilin, two main components of pseudopodia, leading hence to invasiveness impairment. This effect is reinforced by the inositol-induced inhibition on metalloproteinases and ROCK1/2 release reshape the cell architecture (Bizzarri, 2016). Phytic acid also has role to assuage the side effects of breast cancer treatment (Proietti *et al.*, 2017). The antitumor therapies suggest daily consumption of 8-12 g of phytic acid per day whereas 1-2 g have a preventive effect in cancer development (Vucenik *et al.*, 2006).

4. Phytic acid as an Antioxidant

Accumulation of free radicals during flawed metabolic activities leads to cell membrane degradation and antioxidants can overcome this oxidative stress. Phytic acid exhibit robust antioxidant property as result of inhibition of hydroxyl radical formation (Graf and Eton, 1985; 1990). The structure of phytic acid (Inositol hexaphosphate) composed of an inositol ring linked to six phosphate groups where the unique positioning of phosphate at 1,2,3 is axial-equatorial-axial respectively made it liable for specific interaction with iron. This inhibits the formation of hydroxyl radicals.

Abdelaziz *et al.* (2007) reported that microbe induced oxidative stress reduces the peroxidase, superoxide dismutase activity, subsequently enhanced with treatment with phytic acid. Bhowmik *et al.* (2017) reported invitro the phytic acid show iron chelation activity, with the inhibition of iron-induced lipid peroxidation and deoxyribose sugar degrading hydroxyl radicals and thus present an approach that phytic acid can serve as an iron chelator against iron overload diseases like Thalassemia.

5. Phytic acid as Antiplatelet agent

The pathogenesis of thrombosis and atherosclerosis involve adhesion of platelet to endothelial cells, this ensuing release of platelet-derived mediators which leads to platelet aggregation and clotting. Phytic acid exhibit potential to inhibit aggregation of platelets, implying its potential in reduction of risk to cardiovascular disease (Vucenik *et al.*, 1999; Nawrocka *et al.,* 2012).

6. Phytic acid as Antiviral agent

In vitro studies have been carried out to determine the antiviral effect of phytic acid on human immunodeficiency virus. Mallery *et al.* (2019) demonstrated that HIV is crucially dependent upon the host metabolite IP6 to produce infectious virions. Cells deficient in IP6 produce fewer virions, while virions that fail to package sufficient numbers of IP6 molecules are poorly infectious and fail to replicate in primary cells. It has been demonstrated that in MT-4 cells, phytic acid completely repressed the cytopathic effect of HIV and the HIV-specific antigen expression at a concentration of 1.67 mg/ml and phytic acid prevent HIV-1 replication in T cell line (Otake *et al.*, 1989; Otake *et al.*, 1999). Even if the exact mechanism was unclear, perhaps it is stipulated that phytic acid acts on HIV-1 at its early replicative state. Although phytic acid itself be an anti-AIDS drug, it might be explored to offer basis for noteworthy AIDS treatment drug production.

7. Phytic acid as an Antidiabetic remedy

Diabetes is a complicated metabolic disorder either with secretion of defective insulin, flawed insulin secretion or both of them. Hence it results in anomalous increase in blood sugar level (hyperglycemia). Phytic acid rich diet have great significance in lowering the blood glucose level (Yoon *et al.*,1983). Barker *et al.* (1999)

reported that phytic acid regulated insulin secretion by obstructing the action serine-threonine specific protein phosphatase in order to open intracellular calcium channels requisite to release insulin.

In vitro studies by Sanchis *et al.* (2018) showed that ability of phytic acid to chelate metal ions made it significant for treatment of metal catalyzed protein glycosylation which trigger diabetes related diseases. As a result of iron chelate formation by phytate, it blocks Fe^{3+} mediated Advanced Glycation End products (AGEs) formation. These AGEs are supposed to modify the protein structure causing loss of function that leads to the diabetes related diseases development. They further reported that IP6 supplementation lowers the level of circulating AGEs and HbA1c, thereby help to prevent diabetes related diseases.

8. Phytic acid against Renal stone formation

Renal stone are formed when urine contains increased crystal forming substances like calcium, oxalate, uric acid amongst these about 80 % of stones are calcium stones. Under normal crystallization conditions the crystals are flushed out due to small size. However once normal crystallization conditions are disturbed, crystal nucleation and its rate are elevated so that crystal are not flushed out easily due to its increased size (Kumar, 2010). Phytic acid which has ion chelating property, chelate out calcium and make it unavailable for crystallization of calcium and oxalate (Grases and Costa-Bauza, 2019). Thus, the phytic acid holds a potential to reduce the renal stone formation.

9. Phytic acid in Parkinson's and Alzheimer's disease

Phytic acid also has significance to combat the neurodegenerative diseases, because of its iron chelating ability. Parkinson's is progressive neurodegenerative disorder that portray striatal dopamine reduction leads to degeneration of neurons in substantia nigra, implicated in irreversible motor dysfunction (Xu *et al.*, 2011). Although iron is one of essential ion for number of metabolic processes, likewise it ensnares in hydroxyl radical production. The increased level of iron in brain interacts with neuromelanin results in increased oxidative stress and persuade neurodegeneration henceforth reduction of iron concentration in brain might help in dealing with Parkinson's diseases. Xu *et al.* (2011) showed the neuroprotective effect of phytic acid on 6-hydroxydopamine-(6-OHDA-) induced Parkinson's disease in cell cultured model. Thus, the iron chelating ability of phytic acid slowed down the further development of Parkinson's diseases.

Abe and Taniguchi (2014) reported the role of phytic acid in prevention of Alzheimer. Alzheimer disease, a neurodegenerative disorder triggered due to accumulation amyloid-β peptide (Aβ) in brain. Over a successive cleavage by β-secretase 1 (BACE1) and γ-secretase Aβ is obtained from amyloid-β precursor protein. Consequently, inhibition of BSCE1 prevent Aβ accumulation. They reported inhibitory effect of phytic acid and rice digest against BSCE1 in neuroblastoma cells without cytotoxicity. Thus, rice components including IP6 may be hopeful preliminary materials for the development of potent and safe drugs and/or food to prevent Alzheimer disease.

10. Phytic acid in Dentistry

Phytic acid has vast applications in dentistry. IP 6 plays an important role in refining the characteristics of cements useful in dentistry. Cement is required to fix bands, brackets to the teeth and also prevent dental caries throughout dental treatment (Millett *et al.*, 2016). Meininger *et al.* (2017) reported that cytocompatibility of phytic acid containing cements, hydration mechanism and setting kinetics was considerably well than citrate containing cements towards osteoblasts.

In dentistry etching is carried to remove the smear layer that is present after tooth preparation and also it opens the dentinal tubules, demineralizing enough of the dentin to allow the formation of resin tags within the dentin structure. This process in combination with dentin adhesives result in bond strengths adequate to place and retain restorations. Originally phosphoric acid at 37 % used as etching agent. However, it was observed that used of phosphoric acid fallouts in collagen fibrils exposure, devoid of hydroxyapatite (Van Meerbeek *et al.*,1996; De Munck er al., 2003). Nassar *et al.* (2013) compared phytic acid and phosphoric acid as etching agent and reported remarkable increase in the bond strength of resin to dentine as compared to phosphoric acid also it has less side effect om pulpal cells.

In root canal therapy a smear layer develops in the canal wall during debridement which is frequently related to incomplete seal and adaptation of obturation material inside the canal walls. To remove the smear layer chelating agent were used. Muana *et al.* (2020) reported that only 1 % of phytic acid showed remarkably improved roughness and lower microhardness as compared to 17 % EDTA. Phytic acid is also applied as implant surface treating agents to generate a bioactive surface with improved osteointegration and reduction in sticking of biofilm. Beside this phytic acid is often utilized to improve the proficiency of various oral care products.

11. Phytic acid as Antihyperlipidemic agent

Excessive dietary fat consumption indorses obesity and hyperlipidemia provokes increased risk of cardiovascular diseases, fatty liver disease and diabetes mellitus. Dietary supplementation of phytic acid is beneficial for such hyperlipidemia management. Kang *et al.* (2012) reported that supplementation of rice bran and phytic acid through diet negate high fat induced hyperlipidemia, by increasing regulation of lipogenic enzyme activities in high fat fed mice. Okazaki *et al.* (2018) noted fortification of feed with phytic acid downregulates expression of hepatic lipogenic gene and modulate gut microbiota; increased fecal and cecal ratio of *Lactobacillus* sp. in high-sucrose diet fed rat.

12. Phytic acid against Ulcer

Ulcers are sores on skin surface and mucosal lining; that are slow to heal and recurring. Sudheer Kumar *et al.* (2004) reported cytoprotective action phytic acid on gastric mucosa; it effectively reduced the gastric ulcer against ibuprofen, ethanol and cold stress induced ulcer in rat paw edema model. Although phytic acid have few antinutrient characteristic, it has crucial therapeutic role in several disease conditions which overshadow its adverse effect. Indeed, due to its chelating property approve to contribute it as an antioxidant. These therapeutic applications prove that phytic acid is a dynamic constituent with multiple therapeutic values *viz.*, anticancer, anti-inflammatory, antiplatelet, antidiabetic and many more. It also has ability to avert neurodegenerative diseases. Such a vast therapeutic potential of phytic acid prove it as a promising pharmaceutical agent.

13. References

1) Abdelaziz, S., El-Saad, A and Mahmood, M. (2007). Phytic acid exposure alters Aflatoxin B1induced reproductive and oxidative toxicity in albino rats. *Euid Based Complementary and Alternative Medicine*, 6(3): 331 - 341.
2) Abdulwaliyu, I., Arekemase, S. O., Adudu, J. A., Batari, M. L., Egbule, M. N and Reuben Okoduwa, S. I. (2019). Investigation of the Medicinal Significance of Phytic Acid as an Indispensable Anti-nutrientin Diseases. *Clinical Nutrition Experimental*, 12: 1 - 36.
3) Abe, T. K and Taniguichi, M. (2014). Identification of myo-inositol hexakis phosphate 790 (IP6) as a β-791 secretase 1 (BACE 1) inhibitory molecule in rice grain extract and digest. *FEBs Open*792 *Bio,* 4: 162 - 167.
4) Barker, C. J and Berggren, P. O. (1999). Inositol hexakis phosphate and beta-cell stimulus-secretion coupling. *Anticancer Research*,19: 3737 - 3741.

5) Bhowmik, A., Ojha, D., Goswami, D., Das, R., Chandra, N. S., Chatterjee, T. K., Chakravarty, A., Chakravarty, S and Chattopadhyay, D. (2017). Inositol hexaphosphoric acid (phytic acid), a nutraceuticals, attenuates iron-induced oxidative stress and alleviates liver injury in iron overloaded mice. *Biomedical Pharmacology*, 87: 443 – 450.
6) Bizzarri, M., Laganà, A. S., Aragona, D and Unfer, V. (2020). Inositol and pulmonary function. Could myo-inositol treatment down regulate inflammation and cytokine release syndrome in SARS-CoV-2? *European Reviews of Medical Pharmaceutical Sciences*, 24: 3426 - 3432.
7) De Munck, J., Van Meerbeek, B., Yoshida, Y., Inoue, S., Vargas, M., Suzuki, K., Lambrechts P and Vanherle, G. (2003). Four-year water degradation of total-etch adhesives bonded to dentin. *Journal of Dental Research*, 82: 136 – 140.
8) Dvorakova, J. (1998). Phytase: Sources, Preparation and Exploitation. *Folia Microbiology,* 43: 323 - 338.
9) Feil, B. (2001). Phytic acid. *Journal of New Seeds*, 3: 1 - 35.
10) Graf, E and Eaton, J. W. (1985). Dietary suppression of colonic cancer. Fiber or phytate? *Cancer,* 56: 717 – 728.
11) Graf, E and Eaton, J. W. (1990). Antioxidant functions of phytic acid. *Free Radicals and Biological Medicine*, 8: 61 – 69.
12) Grases, F and Costa Bauza, A. (2019). Key Aspects of Myo-Inositol Hexaphosphate (Phytate) and Pathological Calcifications. *Molecules*, 24: 4434 - 4438.
13) Harland, B. F and Morris, E. R. (1995). Phytate: a good or bad food component? *Nutrition Research*, 19: 947 - 961.
14) Kang, M. Y., Kim, S. M., Rico, C. W and Lee, S. C. (2012). Hypolipidemic and antioxidative effects of rice bran and phytic acid in high fat-fed mice. *Food Science and Biotechnology*, 21: 23 - 28.
15) Kim, J. N., Han, S. N and Kim, H. K. (2014). Phytic acid and myo-inositol support adipocyte dierentiation and improve insulin sensitivity in 3T3-L1 cells. *Nutrition Research*, 34: 723 - 731.
16) Kumar, V., Sinha, A. K., Makkar, H and Becker, K. (2010). Dietary roles of phytate and phytase in human nutrition: A review. *Food Chemistry*, 120: 945 – 959.
17) Lott, J. N. A. (1984). Accumulation of seed reserves of phosphorus and other minerals. In Seed Physiology. Development, 139-166 [DR Murray, editor]. London: Academic Press.
18) Manary, M. J., Krebs, N. F., Gibson, R. S., Broadhead, R. L and Hambridge, K. M. (2002). Community-based dietary phytate reduction and its effect on iron status in Malawian children. *Annals of Tropical Perinatology*, 22: 133 -136.

19) Meininger, S., Blum, C., Schamel, M., Barralet, J. E., Ignatius, A and Gbureck, U. (2017). Phytic acid as alternative setting retarder enhanced biological performance of dicalcium phosphate cement *in vitro*. *Science and Reproduction,* 7: 558 – 610.

20) Millett, D. T., Glenny, A. M., Mattick, R. C., Hickman, J., and Mandall, N. A. (2016). Adhesives for fixed orthodontic bands. *Cochrane Database Systemic Reviews*, 10: CD004485.

21) Muana, H. L., Nassar, M., Dargham, A., Hiraishi, N and Tagami, J. (2020). Effect of smear layer removal agents on the microhardness and roughness of radicular dentin. *Saudi Dental Journal*, 10: 1 - 5.

22) Nassar, M., Hiraishi, N., Islam, M. S., Aizawa, M., Tamura, Y., Otsuki, M., Kasugai, S. Ohya K. and Tagam, J. (2013). Effect of phytic acid used as etchant on bond strength, smear layer, and pulpal cells. *European Journal of Oral Science*, 121: 482 - 487.

23) Nawrocka, M. D and Latocha, M. (2012). Phytic acid: Anticancer nutriceutic, Pol. Merkur. *Lekarski*: *Organ Polskiego Towarzystwa Lekarskiego*, 33: 43 - 47.

24) Okazaki, Y., Sekita, A. and Katayama, T. (2018). Intake of phytic acid and myo-inositol lowers hepatic lipogenic gene expression and modulates gut microbiota in rats fed a high-sucrose diet. *Biomedical Reports*, 8: 466 - 474.

25) Otake, T., Mori, H and Morimoto, M. (1999). Anti-HIV-1 activity of myo-inositol hexaphosphoric acid (IP6) and myo-inositol hexasulfate (IS6). *Anticancer Research*, 19: 3723 – 3726.

26) Otake, T., Shimonaka, H and Kanai, M. (1989). Inhibitory effect of inositol hexasulfate and inositol hexaphosphoric acid (phytic acid) on the proliferation of the Human Immunodeficiency Virus (HIV) *in vitro*. *Kansenshogaku Zasshi*, 63: 676 – 683.

27) Pallauf, J and Rimbach, G. (1996). Nutritional significance of phytic acid and phytase. *Archives of Animal Nutrition,* 50: 301 - 319.

28) Proietti, S., Pasta, V., Cucina, A., Aragona, C., Palombi, E and Vucenic, I. (2017). Inositol hexaphosphate (InsP6) as an effective topical treatment for patients receiving adjuvant chemotherapy after breast surgery. *European Reviews of Medical and Pharmacological Science,* 21(2): 43 - 50.

29) Reddy, N. R., Pierson, M. D., Sathe, S. K and Salunkhe, D. K. (1989). Phytates is cereals and legumes. CRC Press, Inc., Boca Raton, Fla.

30) Reddy, N. R., Sathe, S. K and Salunkhe, D. K. (1982). Phytates in legumes and cereals. *Advances in Food Research*, 28: 1 - 91.

31) Sanchis, P., Rivera, R., Berga, F., Fortuny, R., Adrover, M., Costa-Bauza, A., Grases, F. and Masmiquel, L. (2018). Phytate Decreases Formation of Advanced Glycation End-Products in Patients with Type II Diabetes: Randomized Crossover Trial. *Science and Reproduction,* 8: 9619.
32) Sudheer Kumar, M., Sridhar Reddy, B., Kiran Babu, S., Bhilegaonkar, P. M., Shirwaikar, A and Unnikrishnan, M. K. (2004). Anti-inflammatory and antiulcer activities of phytic acid in rats. *Indian Journal of Experimental Biology*, 42: 179 - 185.
33) Van Meerbeek, B., Conn, L. J., Jr., Duke, E. S., Eick, J. D., Robinson, S. J., and Guerrero, D. (1996). Correlative transmission electron microscopy examination of non-demineralized and demineralized resin-dentin interfaces formed by two dentin adhesive systems. *Journal of Dental Research*, 75: 879 - 888.
34) Vucenik, I and Shamsuddin, A. M. (2006). Protection against cancer by dietary IP6 and inositol. *Nutrition and Cancer*, 55: 109 – 125.
35) Vucenik, I., Podczasy, J. J and Shamsuddin, A. M. (1099). Antiplatelet activity of inositol hexaphosphate (IP6). *Anticancer Research*, 19(5A): 3689 - 3693.
36) Xu, Q., Kanthasamy, G and Reddy, M. B. (2011). Phytic Acid Protects against 6-Hydroxydopamine-Induced Dopaminergic Neuron Apoptosis in Normal and Iron Excess Conditions in a Cell Culture Model. Parkinson's Disease, Volume 2011, Article ID 431068, 6 pages.
37) Yoon, J. H., Thompson, L. U and Jenkins, D. J. (1983). The effect of phytic acid on *in vitro* rate of starch digestibility and blood glucose response. *American Journal of Clinical Nutrition*, 38: 835 - 842.

Advances in Pharmaceutical Science
ISBN: 978-81-951323-7-9
First Edition; Volume – 1; 2021
Chapter – 2, Page: 11 - 17

2

PHARMACOLOGIC DRUGS FROM NATURAL SOURCES

Remya Madan Gopal*

Pillai HOC College of Arts, Science and Commerce, Rasayani, Navi, Mumbai, Maharashtra, India

*Corresponding author: remyagopal@mes.ac.in

Abstract

Since time immemorial, humans have instinctively explored their natural surroundings to find ways to mitigate, alleviate and cure the maladies, injuries and ailments that afflict them. Rational drug design is a fairly recent development and even then, more often than not, most synthetically derived drugs trace their origin to some natural source wherein the synthetic product is a derivatised or modified form of the naturally extracted compound. Natural sources of pharmacologically important drugs can be plants, animals, microbes, minerals or the newfound and unique marine sources. Here, an attempt has been made to give a snapshot of these varied sources of drugs and each category is dealt with briefly. The compendium of naturally derived drugs is very vast and the reader is advised to search the available literature if detailed and concise information is needed on any particular source of interest.

Key words: Drugs, Pharmacology, Natural products and Plant sources.

1. Introduction

People have relied upon nature for their straightforward necessities just like the hotspots for prescriptions, covers, food stuffs, scents, clothing, flavors, manures and methods for transportation all through the ages. A drug, according to WHO definition, is any substance or product that is used or intended to be used to modify or explore the physiological system or pathological state in the benefit of the recipient. Development of a new drug usually takes one or more of these four routes:

a) Modification of an existing approved drug.
b) Random high throughput screening for biologic activity of large numbers of natural products, banks of previously discovered chemical entities or large libraries of organic molecules.
c) Rational computer-aided drug design (CADD) based on an understanding of biologic mechanisms and chemical structure.
d) Biotechnology and cloning tools

Historically, for ages, natural products have contributed to the development of new pharmaceutical drugs; approximately 50 % of all small-molecule drugs have a natural product derivation or inspiration. This would seem a pragmatic approach due to the tremendous diversity of natural products in nature.

As Frank Lovering had noted about stereo-chemical complexity in drug development, modern day rational drug design is also benefitted by the vast reservoir of complex structural information contained in many of the natural products. With the development of science of chemical analysis, the actual pharmacological active principle of the drug from the natural sources could be identified as also the mechanism of action in the body. Sertürner purified morphine from poppy in 1804 and observed that opium's analgesic and sedative effects were reproduced by morphine. This paved way for others to find the active pharmaceutical ingredient (API) of the drug, for example, quinine from cinchona, cocaine from cocoetc. Further development in chemistry led to structural elucidation of the drugs and thus, we could also chemically synthesize the drug or make suitable modifications to enhance its pharmacological properties and effects.

The number of pharmacologically effective compounds that are derived from various sources is vast but the limiting factor for the actual clinical use of these compounds is more often than not, unfavorable toxic, pharmacokinetic and pharmacodynamic properties that lead to failure in clinical trials. Solubility of drugs for proper absorption is always a problem to surmount and there may be limitations to the kind of chemical modifications that may be introduced on the API for modifying it for suitable and useful properties and safety profiles. Modern drug development is a multi-billion dollar industry involving huge cost inputs but also huge returns for a successfully marketed drug. The cost and time factors involved in a new drug development and marketing has concentrated the actual drug market to a few select pharmaceutical companies referred to as Big Pharma. High Throughput Screening (HTS) and Computer Aided Drug Design (CADD) are now a routine part of rational drug design process that has contributed in bringing down drug development costs and simplified to some extent the needle in a haystack conundrum of drug design and development. Natural sources of drugs may be broadly divided into plant sources, animal sources, microbial sources, mineral sources and semi-synthetic sources. We will look in detail into each of these sources below.

2. Plant Sources

Among the natural sources of drugs, plants are the most important and major sources of all drugs. Many plant species have known pharmacological properties. Initially, only leaves were used but now, all plant tissue parts are used and the pharmacologic properties may be due to their phyto-constituents such as glycosides, alkaloids, saponins, oils, waxes, gums and mucilages, resins, toxins, steroids, flavonoids, tannins, and terpenoids. Plant extracts may be used directly as crude drugs or further processed. Drugs from plants exert various biological activities including virucidal, bactericidal, fungicidal, anti-inflammatory, analgesic, sedative, spasmolytic, and local anesthetic activities among others. A few categories of active principle agents from above are mentioned. Alkaloids- these are mostly plant derived but some are of animal origin. They are called alkaloids because they are 'alkali-like'. Name of alkaloid-based drugs are usually suffixed with 'ine' Some important alkaloids are:

a) Xanthine alkaloids: Caffeine
b) Opium alkaloids: Morphine
c) Cocaine alkaloids: Cocaine
d) Cinchona alkaloids: Quinine
e) Vinca alkaloids: Vinblastine
f) Belladona alkaloids: Atropine

Glycosides are crystalline solids composed of a sugar and non-sugar component. Pharmacological activity lies with the non-sugar component while the sugar component largely determines the pharmacokinetic properties. Digoxin, salicylic acid, digitoxin etc. are examples of glycosides.

Oils from plant sources are divided into essential oils and fixed oils. Essential oils usually contain aromatic volatile compounds that evaporate without leaving a stain like clove oil and peppermint oil. Fixed oils are higher fatty acids and triglycerides like castor oil, olive oil etc. Waxes are esters of higher fatty acids. Gums and mucilages are complex polysaccharides. Resins are bitter, insoluble polymers of volatile oils for example as a foetida. Tannins are non-nitrogenous, bitter phenolic derivatives.

3. Animal sources

Animal sources of drugs may be obtained from the whole organism, a specific part or organ or they may be glandular secretions. For example, cod liver oil is obtained from the liver of Gadus spp. Hirudin is obtained from H. medicinalis and heparin from H. manillensis.

4. Microbial sources

Many important antibiotics and life-saving drugs have been obtained from microbes. Alexander Fleming created history when he discovered penicillin, the first antimicrobial drug. Antibiotics are not the only class of drugs obtained from microbial sources. The repertoire of drugs now encompasses anticancer, lipid lowering, immunosuppressant, anti-infective, anti-atopic etc.

5. Semi-synthetic Drugs

One of the ways mentioned earlier for obtaining a new drug is to modify the properties of an existing approved drug. Many drugs obtained from natural sources can be further chemically altered and modified to impart novel and more effective pharmacological properties.

6. Marine Natural Products

An emerging and novel source of therapeutic agents is from marine sources that have distinct mechanisms of action. The limited accessibility and amount of material obtained from marine organisms had so far stunted the development of therapeutic products from these sources. Structural, chemical and biological elucidation of the compounds has made it possible to study in detail the unique therapeutic potentials of marine natural products. Scale up synthesis has now allowed drugs from marine sources to hit the market and many of them are undergoing clinical trials.

7. Antineoplastic Drugs: A special note

Cancer remains the biggest reason for morbidity and majority of drug development activities by the big pharma is directed towards finding a panacea for the same. Natural products derived anti-neoplastic drugs form a major chunk of drugs that are either obtained from natural sources or they are modified versions of some anticancer natural product. The sources are varied although maximum drugs are obtained from plants. Some of the important anti- cancer drugs obtained from natural sources are the Vinca alkaloids, taxanes, camptothecin, combretastatin, colchicine, etoposide, paclitaxel (Taxol®), docetaxel, topotecan, and irinotecan, salvicine, ellipticine, roscovitine, maytanasin, etc. Among the many microbial metabolites with anticancer properties, taxol, doxorubicin, daunorubicin, bleomycin, actinomycin D etc. are among the most important of the cancer chemotherapeutic agents.

8. Conclusion

Modern drug development depends to a great extent on high throughput screening (HTS) to find hits rummaging through chemical libraries previously synthesized or the drug design route goes through rational drug design process through computer aided drug design (CADD) in the event that structure of the druggable target protein or the ligand or both is known through X-ray crystallography or NMR. Although the methods to analyze best possible drug candidates has improved substantially, the number of drugs hitting the market is quite few. It has of course to do with safety and compatibility profile of the drugs and the stringent regulations defining safety concerns. After a dip in the past due to modern drug designing processes, the use of natural product compounds has now slowly gathered momentum recently with a better understanding of signaling pathways and also because of better lead compounds being obtained from natural sources.

9. References

1) Alberti F, Foster GD and Bailey AM. (2017). Natural products from filamentous fungi and production by heterologous expression. Applied Microbiology and Biotechnology, 101(2): 493 - 500.
2) Atanasov AG, Waltenberger B and Pferschy Wenzig EM. (2015). Discovery and resupply of pharmacologically active plant-derived natural products: A review. Biotechnology Advances, 33(8): 1582 - 1614.
3) Azab A, Nassar A and Azab AN. (2016). Anti-Inflammatory Activity of Natural Products. Molecules, 21(10): 1321 - 1330.
4) Beutler JA. (2019). Natural Products as a Foundation for Drug Discovery. Current Protocols in Pharmacology, 86(1): e67.
5) Burns DC, Mazzola EP and Reynolds WF. (2019). The role of Computer-Assisted Structure Elucidation (CASE) programs in the structure elucidation of complex natural products. Natural Products and Reproduction, 36(6): 919 - 933.
6) Chikara S, Nagaprashantha LD, Singhal J, Horne D, Awasthi S and Singhal SS. (2018). Oxidative stress and dietary phytochemicals: Role in cancer chemoprevention and treatment. Cancer Letters, 413: 122 - 134.
7) Christy MP, Uekusa Y, Gerwick L and Gerwick WH. (2021). Natural Products with Potential to Treat RNA Virus Pathogens Including SARS-CoV-2. Journal of Natural Products, 84(1): 161 - 182.

8) Cragg GM and Pezzuto JM. (2016). Natural Products as a Vital Source for the Discovery of Cancer Chemotherapeutic and Chemopreventive Agents. Medical Principles and Practices, 25(2): 41 - 59.
9) Da Rocha AB, Lopes RM and Schwartsmann G. (2001). Natural products in anticancer therapy. Current Opinion in Pharmacology, 1(4): 364 - 369.
10) Gezici S and Şekeroğlu N. (2019). Current Perspectives in the Application of Medicinal Plants Against Cancer: Novel Therapeutic Agents. Anticancer Agents and Medical Chemistry, 19(1): 101 - 111.
11) Hanif N, Murni A, Tanaka C and Tanaka J. (2019). Marine Natural Products from Indonesian Waters. Marine Drugs, 17(6): 364 - 370.
12) Kalkreuter E, Pan G, Cepeda AJ and Shen B. (2020). Targeting Bacterial Genomes for Natural Product Discovery. Trends in Pharmacological Science, 41(1): 13 - 26.
13) Katz L and Baltz RH. (2016). Natural product discovery: past, present, and future. Journal of Indian Microbiology and Biotechnology, 43(2-3): 155 - 176.
14) Khalifa SAM, Elias N and Farag MA. (2019). Marine Natural Products: A Source of Novel Anticancer Drugs. Marine Drugs, 17(9): 491 - 500.
15) Ma L, Zhang M, Zhao R, Wang D, Ma Y and Li A. (2021). Plant Natural Products: Promising Resources for Cancer Chemoprevention. Molecules, 26(4): 933 - 940.
16) Mondal S, Bandyopadhyay S, Ghosh MK, Mukhopadhyay S, Roy S and Mandal C. (2012). Natural products: promising resources for cancer drug discovery. Anticancer Agents and Medical Chemistry, 12(1): 49 - 75.
17) Morais MC, Souza JV and da Silva Maia Bezerra. (2020). Trypanocidal Essential Oils: A Review. Molecules, 25(19): 4568 - 4575.
18) Nugroho AE and Morita H. (2019). Computationally-assisted discovery and structure elucidation of natural products. Journal of Natural Medicine, 73(4): 687 - 695.
19) Orlikova B, Legrand N, Panning J, Dicato M and Diederich M. (2014). Anti-inflammatory and anticancer drugs from nature. Cancer Treatment and Research, 159: 123 - 143.
20) Sarmento-Neto JF, do Nascimento LG, Felipe CF and de Sousa DP. (2015). Analgesic Potential of Essential Oils. Molecules, 21(1): E20 – E28.
21) Scuteri D, Hamamura K and Sakurada T. (2021). Efficacy of Essential Oils in Pain: A Systematic Review and Meta-Analysis of Preclinical Evidence. Frontiers in Pharmacology, 12: 640128.
22) Singh M, Sharma P, Singh PK, Singh TG and Saini B. (2020). Medicinal Potential of Heterocyclic Compounds from Diverse Natural Sources for the Management of Cancer. Mini Reviews in Medical Chemistry, 20(11): 942 - 957.
23) Sukmarini L. (2021). Recent Advances in Discovery of Lead Structures from Microbial Natural Products: Genomics and Metabolomics - Guided Acceleration. Molecules, 26(9): 2542 - 2550.

24) Thomford NE, Senthebane DA, Rowe A, Munro D, Seele P, Maroyi A and Dzobo K. (2018). Natural Products for Drug Discovery in the 21st Century: Innovations for Novel Drug Discovery. International Journal of Molecular Science, 19(6): 1578 - 1585.
25) Waltenberger B, Mocan A, Šmejkal K, Heiss EH and Atanasov AG. (2016). Natural Products to Counteract the Epidemic of Cardiovascular and Metabolic Disorders. Molecules, 21(6): 807 - 818.
26) Zhang MM, Qiao Y, Ang EL and Zhao H. (2017). Using natural products for drug discovery: the impact of the genomics era. Expert Opinion in Drug Discovery, 12(5): 475 - 487.

Advances in Pharmaceutical Sciences
ISBN: 978-81-951323-7-9
First Edition; Volume – 1; 2021
Chapter – 3, Page: 18 - 37

3

ACTINOBACTERIA - A TREASURE HOUSE OF UNEXPLORED BIOMOLECULES

Reshma Ayswaria[1*] and Parimala Gnana Soundari Arockiam Jeyasundar[2*]

[1]Microboilte Research and Development Private Limited, Bioincubator, Government of Karnataka, Manipal, India

[2]Centre for Futures Studies, Gandhigram Rural Institute-Deemed to be University, Gandhigram, Tamil Nadu, India

*Corresponding author: reshmapkd1991@gmail.com

Abstract

Pharmacological products are reported for their use from ancient time onwards considering their efficacy and safety. Several products are available in the market were reported from plants, animals, and microbes. Actinobacteria are Gram-positive microbes, sharing the properties of both bacteria and fungi which is ubiquitous. A lot of biotechnological products which are having wide applications in our day-to-day life were reported from *Streptomyces* sp. the predominant population of actinobacteria. Metabolite production and species diversity highly influenced by environmental factors. Actinobacteria can be isolated from many sources and the commonly used medium for isolation is Starch Casein Nitrate (SCN) agar medium, the favorable growth condition is at 27 °C for 15 days and the powdery pinpointed colonies will consider for further studies. The use of molecular methods, mycelium and pigment production characterization using International Streptomyces Project (ISP) medium, coverslip method of microscopic observation, and cell wall composition analysis are the few methods of strain identification. Many researchers have reported the use of wide-spectrum use of metabolites for various applications and yet need to carry out further research for the use of unexplored sources. The current book chapter discusses in detail about the various metabolites reported from actinobacteria, its identification, purification, characterization, and applications in the pharma field.

Key words: Actinobacteria, Antimicrobials, Antidiabetic agents Antioxidants, Anticancer & tumor medicines and Pigments

1. Introduction

Actinobacteria considered to be the largest taxonomic unit, the name derived from two Greek words aktis and mukes. Gram positive bacteria with high G+C content in genetic material have mycelium and are reproduced by sporulation (Ludwig *et al.*, 2012). They are ubiquities in nature, present in terrestrial and aquatic ecosystems (Ventura *et al.*, 2007). A lot of biotechnological products which is having wide application in human day to day life are reported including enzymes, pigments, proteins, antibiotics, plant growth promoters, etc. The population of actinobacteria highly influenced by environmental factors, the major population can isolate from soil samples (Williams and Vickers,1989). Commonly they are mesophilic, between 25 and 30°C they can grow, thermophilic will grow at 50 to 60 °C. The proffered range of pH between 6 to 9, and maximum growth recorded at pH 7, less number were isolated from acidic range (Kim *et al.*, 1997). Actinobacteria consist of 5 subclasses, 6 orders, and 14 suborders (Ludwig *et al.*, 2012). The phylum actinobacteria divided into six classes based on 16S rRNA sequencing details which include *Actinobacteria, Acidimicrobiia, Coriobacteriia, Nitriliruptoria, Rubrobacteria* and *Thermoleophilia* and the class *Actinobacteria* consist of 16 orders (Gao and Gupta, 2012).

Microscopic morphology detail serves the initial data for the identification comprising mycelia morphology, spore chain morphology, and production of pigments (Labeda, 1987). Mycelia growth is divided into two different ways aerial and substrate mycelium which is growing upward and downward directions respectively (Flärdh and Buttner, 2009; van Dissel *et al.*, 2014). Spores will grow at aerial mycelium or substrate mycelium as single or group, based on the morphology it is classified as smooth, warty, spiny, hairy, or rugose surfaces (Dietz and Mathews, 1971). Spore chain and its length also one of the characteristic feature for the classification, based on the morphology it is grouped as flexuous (Rectus-Flexibilis), open loops (Relinaculam-Apertum), open or closed spirals (spira), or verticillate (Pridham *et al.*, 1958). Actinobacteria is well known for its pigment production either it is diffusible or non-diffusible pigments (Lechevalier and Lechevalier, 1965). Few of them are reported for melanin production, which is a pigment within the black to brown colour range (Dastager *et al.*, 2006; Manivasagan *et al.*, 2013).

Chemotaxis classification is the next method of identification; this is based on cell wall composition, presence of different amino acids, sugars, and proteins (Goodfellow and Donnell, 1989). Bacterial fatty acids range in chain length from two (C2) to over 90 (C90) carbon atoms, which were reported in actinobacteria. Different types of isoprenoid quinines were reported actinobacteria, menaquinones are the predominant ones in the cell wall (Kroppenstedt, 1985; Suzuki *et al.*, 1993; Collins *et al.*, 1985; Collins, 1994). Based on the presence of sugars the actinobacteria are grouped into cell wall types A to D, which is having different combinations of sugars present in the cell wall. Group A consists arabinose and galactose, group B reported with madurose (3-O-methyl-D-galactose), group C reported with the absence of sugars, group D reported with arabinose and xylose and group E observed with galactose and rhamnose (Labeda, 1987; Lechevalier and Lechevalier, 1970).

Molecular classification includes different genus with unique properties, which includes the genus *Tropheryma* with a GC content of only 46 % and genome size 925, 938 bp (Bentley *et al.*, 2003), the genus *Propionibacterium*, commonly present in skin of humans as commensal and end product of metabolism is propionic acid (Desnues *et al.*, 2010), the genus *Micromonospora*, highly reported as plant growth promoting metabolite producer observed in nodules as endophytes (Hirsch and Valdés, 2009), the genus *Salinispora* the first genus reported for its growth in sea water (Bose *et al.*, 2014), the genus *Mycobacterium* consist *M. bovis* and *M. tuberculosis*, cause disease in immunocompromised people (Jacobson and Krahenbuhl ,1999), the genus *Nocardia* always cause opportunistic infection mainly caused by the inhalation of spores (Abreu *et al.*, 2015), the genus *Corynebacterium* well known representative is *C. glutamicum* used for glutamic acid production (Leuchtenberger *et al.*, 2015), the genus *Gordonia* this can isolate from soil and very rare from sputum samples of patients who is having pulmonary disease (Tsukamura,1971), the genus *Rhodococcus* very close to *Nocardia*, common pathogen of plant and animals (Bell *et al.*, 1998), the genus *Leifsonia* non spore forming and DL-2,4-diaminobutyric acid in their peptidoglycan layer (Janssen *et al.*, 2002), the genus *Bifidobacterium* different shapes will exhibit by the members of this group includes curved, short, and bifurcated Y shapes (Orla-Jensen,1924), the genus *Gardnerella*, present in vaginal discharge, responsible sexually transmitted disease (Kim *et al.*, 2009), the genus *Streptomyces* commonly available most of the biotechnology products were reported from this genus, they are rich in soil (164), the genus *Frankia* which is in symbiotic association and helping for nitrogen fixation and GC content of 72 to 73 % (Ventura *et al.*, 2007).

2. Metabolites and its Applications

Several plant growth promoters were reported from actinobacteria, which include bioherbicide and bioinsecticide. Mildiomycin is an antifungal agent for plants and inhibits protein synthesis of fungus and protects plants (Shivlata, and Satyanarayana, 2017; Swarnalakshmi *et al.*, 2016). *S. hygroscopicus*, produced a metabolite used as plant growth promoters with auxin-like activity (Igarashi, 2004). Different enzymes with industrial application also reported from actinobacteria few of them are xylanases, amylase, and cellulase by Streptomyces sp. Different pharma products are also available in the market includes Nystatin anti-fungal agent, tetracyclin as anti-bacterial, Spectinomycin as anti-tuberculosis, aoronamycin as an anti-malarial agent, Strepturidin for immunotherapy, Xiamycin as anti-HIV, Belomycin is an antitumor, etc. Similarly, it is also produced different pigments and biosurfactants (Reshma *et al.*, 2020), these are widely used in the pharma, cosmetic and detergent industry respectively.

3. Antioxidants from Actinobacteria

Antioxidants are substances that can inhibit oxidation and free radicals formation which damages the cells. Based on the functioning property, they are of three main types: primary antioxidants, secondary and tertiary antioxidants. The primary group terminates antioxidants formation, the second group converts hyperoxide molecules to nonreactive heat-stable molecules and the final group repairs the damaged molecules using phenotypic enzymes, enzymes of DNA, etc. Vitamins C and E, selenium, and carotenoids, such as beta-carotene, lycopene, lutein, and zeaxanthin are the common antioxidants.

Rhizosphere soil samples of *Magnolia singapurensis* and *Angelonia angustifolia* were collected for actinobacteria isolation and fifty-one isolates were identified. These isolates were screened for antibacterial and antioxidant activities. *S. aureus* InaCC-B4 and *E. coli* InaCC-B5 were selected as test pathogens. After two weeks of incubation, ethyl acetate extract was used for the extraction of metabolites, and separated fractions were used for different assays. DPPH assay, MIC value, antibacterial activity, and TLC autobiography were performed for the characterization of extract. TN01-27 and TN01-17 were confirmed with good antioxidant activity (Praptiwi *et al.*, 2019). Endophytic actinomycetes are the group of microbes that is present inside the plant leaf, root, or stem. *Vochysia divergens* is a Brazilian medicinal plant used for the isolation of endophytic actinobacteria and confirmed its metabolite production for antitumor, antioxidant, and antimicrobial activities. Molecular studies identified the isolates belongs to *Microbispora* sp., *Streptomyces sampsonii*, and *Micromonospora* sp. Folin–Ciocalteau method was used for phenolic estimation and the DPPH assay was used for the confirmation of antioxidant activity of phenol compounds. *Streptomyces sampsonii* extract 0.000337 mg/g and extract from *Microbispora* sp., 228.6364 mg/g were identified with good antioxidant activity (Savi *et al.*, 2015).

Streptomyces carpaticus MK-01 was isolated from the marine region and tested for its antimicrobial, antioxidant, and cytotoxic effect by Subramanian *et al.*, (2017). About 24 isolates were subjected for the study and MK-01 ethyl acetate extract shows good antioxidant activity. Yeast Malt Extract (ISP 2) medium used for the cultivation for a week time and beta-carotene bleaching assay was performed for antioxidant property analysis. *S. carpaticus* MK-01 was identified as the potential strain for antioxidant activity. Antioxidant-producing actinobacteria from the terrestrial region was isolated by Jessy Padma *et al.* (2018). From two different soil samples, fifteen isolates were identified and molecular studies confirmed that strains belonged to actinomycetes and TS 1010 was identified as a potential strain. Dot-blot assay and DPPH assay were performed for the rapid scavenging activity confirmation of metabolites for all the isolates.

Actinobacteria isolated from marine sediments collected from the Kakinada coast used for antioxidant and antiproliferative metabolite production screening. Three different medium were used for isolation including Starch Casein Agar, Chitin Agar, Glycerol Asparagine Agar respectively followed by two weeks of incubation at 28 °C. Results of biochemical, morphological, and molecular studies confirmed that isolates belong to actinobacteria later the methanolic extraction was performed and the organic layer evaporated at 70 °C from bioactive isolate. The collected extract dissolved in 5 % DMSO and DPPH assay followed by FRAP assay were performed. The DPPH assay was performed at 20 – 100 μg/ml concentration, superoxide activity of the same extract confirmed as 35 μg/ml, and FRAP assay results concluded that increasing concentration supporting improved antioxidant activity (Nagaseshu *et al.*, 2016).

Nocardiopsis alba isolated from mangrove soil collected from Andhra Pradesh, and its potential role for antioxidant production was screened. DPPH assay and reducing the power of the sample was estimated for the antioxidant assay. HPLC, NMR, FTIR were used for structure elucidation (Janaradhan *et al.*, 2014). Rhizosphere soil of a Caatinga plant was selected for isolation and these were collected from Northeastern Brazil. *Glutamicibacter*, *Mycobacterium, Nocardiopsis*, and main Streptomyces were isolated from the region. TAA and DPPH assay were performed for antioxidant activities (de Moura *et al.*, 2021). Endophytic actinobacteria was isolated from *Holothuria leucospilota* and its metabolite used for antioxidant activity study. This plant was collected from Larak Island, Persian Gulf, and Starch Casein Nitrate (SCN) agar medium used for the isolation. Among seventeen isolates *Streptomyces* sp. strain SC 156 was identified as a potential strain for antioxidant metabolite production through DPPH assay later molecular study reveals that the strain was more similar with *S. chartreusis* (Gozari *et al.*, 2018).

Marine *Streptomyces* sp. S2A was isolated by Siddharth and Vittal (2018) and its metabolites were used for enzyme inhibition, antioxidant, antimicrobial, and cytotoxic studies. DPPH (0.86 mg), ABTS (11.77 μg), FRAP, and metal chelating activity (0.25 – 2 mg/Ml) of metabolite were checked for antioxidant property confirmation. The molecular study reveals that the strain belongs to Streptomyces sp. and identified as *Streptomyces griesoruber. Saccharothrix ecbatanensis* UTMC 537 was tested for multiple metabolite production for antioxidant activity. DPPH assay was performed for the confirmation and methanolic extract was used for the assay. Different properties include super oxidase activity, xanthaine oxidase property, and lipoxygenase activity was assessed for antioxidant activity (Mohammadipanah and Momenilandi, 2018).

4. Pigments from Actinobacteria

Bacterial pigments are the groups extracted from plants or microbes and widely used in the food, pharma, dyeing, and cosmetic industries. Biodegradability and biocompatibility are the main attractive functions of biopigments. Pigment from marine actinobacteria was screened against *Staphylococcus aureus, Pseudomonas aeruginosa, Bacillus subtilis, Escherichia coli, Salmonella typhi* by Udhyakumar *et al.*, (2017) and more susceptible towards, *Escherichia coli.* Similarly, antifungal activity was confirmed with *Candida albicans, Aspergillus niger, Trichoderma viride, Rhizopus microporous,* and more effective against *A. niger.* Collected soil samples were serially diluted and plating was performed by using Starch Casein Agar followed by incubation at 27 °C for 3 - 7 days. Biochemical and molecular tests were performed for the identification of the strains followed by FITR analysis of pigments. A total of 55 isolates were observed and 17 were selected as potential strain and most efficacies were reported with *Streptomyces rochei* with NH and NOH functional group. Kamarudheen *et al.* (2019) collected marine soil samples from the Arabian Sea, Allepey, Kerala, India. *Nocardiopsis dassonvillei* was identified as a potential strain with melanin production and its efficacy was tested against human pathogens. The presence of melanin was confirmed using UV-Visible spectrophotometry and Fourier Transfer Infra-Red spectroscopy. Starch Casein Agar, Actinomycetes Isolation Agar, Tyrosine Agar Base (ISP7), M1 media were used for the isolation, and melanin production was determined by using Peptone Yeast Extract Iron agar

(ISP6) and Tyrosine Agar Base (ISP7). Finally, the quorum quenching property of melanin was studied using the same pathogens concluded that this pigment can be used to control biofilm formation.

Eighty-seven soil samples were collected from Iran and used for actinobacteria isolation followed by serial dilution on Starch Casein Agar and Yeat Malt Extract (ISP2) medium. The pigment was subjected to antimicrobial activity test against *Staphylococcus aureus, Bacillus cereus, Escherichia coli, Pseudomonas aeruginosa, Shigella dysenteries, Citrobacter ferundii, Klebsiella pneumoniae, Serratia marcescens*, *Aspergillus* sp. and *Candida albicans*. The bioactive strain was confirmed as *Streptomyces coeruleorubidus* and more inhibition was observed against *Staphylococcus aureus* and resistance was recorded against *Aspergillus* sp., *Candida albicans* and *Escherichia coli* (Azimi *et al*., 2014). Rhizosphere soil samples were collected from Madhya Pradesh state used for isolation of actinobacteria. A total of 85 strains were reported and 5 observed with pigment production. Methanol extraction was performed and later the antimicrobial properties of the samples were screened against multiple pathogens. Mass Spectrometry and Nuclear Magnetic Resonance Spectroscopy analysis was used for the profiling of pigment (Parmar and Singh, 2018).

Soil samples for actinobacteria isolation were collected from the Kovalam Beach regions of Chennai, Tamil Nadu, India. Out of 4 isolates, only 1 reported pigment production. Ethyl acetate was used for the extraction, followed by FTIR, GC-MS, and HPLC characterization of pigment. Antibacterial activity of the pigment identified and optimized condition for enhanced production observed as 35 ^{o}C – 40 ^{o}C and optimal pH was found to between 6.0 and 8.0 (Srinivasan *et al*., 2017). *Streptomyces* sp. JAR6 was identified as a bioactive strain with red pigment production. Starch Casein Nitrate medium used for isolation and Yeast Extract-Malt Extract agar medium used for the subculturing. Good inhibition was observed against *Salmonella* sp., *Proteus mirabilis*, *Shigella* sp. and *Enterococcus* sp. and less activity recorded with *Staphylococcus aureus*, *Klebsiella pneumonia*, and *Escherichia coli* (Abraham and Chauhan, 2018).

Pigment extracted from *Streptomyces parvulus* C5-5Y checked for its antimicrobial property by Soundari *et al*. (2017). Soil samples for isolation was collected from leather industry region of Vellore, Tamilnadu. Starch Casein Nitrate (SCN) medium used for the isolation and screening was performed again wide range of microbes *viz*., *Staphylococcus aureus, Staphylococcus epidermidis, Enterococcus* sp., *Escherichia coli, Pseudomonas aeruginosa, Klebsiella pneumoniae, Salmonella typhi, Proteus* sp., *Shigella* sp., *Bacillus* sp., *and Candida albicans*. Characterization of pigment was done by using UV spectrophotometry, TLC, HPTLC and LC-MS/MS.

5. Antimicrobial agents from Actinobacteria

Antimicrobials are the drugs used to suppress or inhibit the growth of microbes and called bacteriostatic or bactericidal agents. The mechanism of these agents either by a disturbing cell wall, protein synthesis, or by damaging DNA or RNA, etc. Marine soil samples were collected by Abd-Elnaby *et al.* (2015) and screened against five bacterial pathogens using metabolites from seventeen actinobacterial isolates. The strain *Streptomyces parvus* identified using 16S rRNA sequencing and considered as bioactive isolate against *Staphylococcus aureus, Escherichia coli, Pseudomonas aeruginosa, and Aeromonas hydrophila* respectively. The metabolite production was optimized by Plackett Burman and equal volume of chloroform, n-butanol, and ethyl acetate was used for extraction. Gas Chromatography (GC) used for the profiling of metabolites and identified as ethane, 1,1-diethoxy; di-n-octyl phthalate; ethanol, 2,2-diethoxy; 9,12-octadecadienoic acid; methyl ester (E, E), and benzoic acid. Actinobacteria with a predominant population of Streptomyces was isolated from the moon milk sample from the cave region. International *Streptomyces* Project medium 5 (ISP 5) was used for the isolation of actinobacteria. Cross streak method was performed for screening against *Klebsiella pneumoniae, E. coli, C. freundii, P. aeruginosa, S. aureus, B. subtilis* and *M. luteus*. All the bioactive isolates from actinobacteria were identified with PKS-I, PKSII, and PKSIII (Adam *et al.*, 2018).

Fungus growing termites were selected as the source of actinobacteria isolation and ninety-seven actinobacteria isolates were discovered in 2018 by René Benndorf *et al.* (2018). The test pathogens were selected from both Gram positive and Gram negative group, later the structure elucidation identified the active compound as rubrominins A and B. *Streptomyces* sp. from the root of *Zingiber officinale* and *Alpinia galanga* was isolated and identified for it is effective antagonism against *Candida albicans* by Taechowisan and Lumyong (2003). Araujo *et al.* (2000) reported *Streptomyces* sp. from maize and reported its antibacterial and antifungal activity. *Azadiracha indica* plant was used for the selection of *Streptomyces* sp. and activity confirmed towards *P. fluorescence.* Ezra *et al.* (2004) reported endophytic *Streptomyces* sp., against *Cryptococcus neoformans* and *Plasmodium falcieparum.* Passari *et al.* (2017) reported twelve numbers of *Streptomyces* sp. able to suppress penicillin-resistant *Staphylococcus aureus*. Tanvir *et al.* (2014) reported Larvicidal activity of these strains were isolated from *Artemisia herbaalba*. Actinomycin D was derived from Streptomyces sp. TCO22 with antifungal activity (Taechowisan and Lumyong,

2003). Munambicins E4, E5, and A-D from endophytic Streptomyces are highly useful against a broad range of Gram positive and Gram negative bacteria (Castillo *et al.* 2002). Roy and Banerjee (2015) reported endophytic *S. rochei* CH1 isolated from Cinnamomum sp. with antibacterial activity against *Aeromonas caviae* and *Vibrio paeachemolyticus*.

Samples were collected from the coastal area of Andaman and Nicobar and isolation was performed using Starch Casein Nitrate (SCN) agar (Usha *et al.*, 2018). Both bacterial and fungal species were used for isolation including *Staphylococcus aureus, Bacillus subtilis, Escherichia coli, Pseudomonas aeruginosa, Streptococcus faecalis, Proteus vulgaris, Rhizopus* sp. *Aspergillus niger, Penicillium notatum, Mucor* sp. using single streak method. Out of sixty-four strains, 32.8 % reported antimicrobial activity, 18.8 % with antibacterial activity, 24.3 % with antifungal, and 14.1 % with an antibacterial with antifungal activity. Samples for isolation were collected from the forest region of India, Northeast region and 172 isolates were discovered. Antibacterial compounds like 2,5-bis(1,1-dimethylethyl) phenol, benzene acetic acid, and nalidixic acid were identified from these strains.

Actinobacteria isolated from marine soil sample was used for the screening of antifungal metabolite production by Soundari *et al.* (2017). Around 30 isolates were identified and five were selected for further study as potential microbes for effective metabolite production. International *Streptomyces* Project (ISP 1-7) medium used for characterization of isolates. The isolates were identified as *Streptomyces sampsonii, Streptomyces tanashiensis, Streptomyces* sp., *Actinoalloteichus cyanogriseus* and *Streptomyces griseus*.

6. Antidiabetic agents from Actinobacteria

The medicines which help to reduce blood sugar in the body of a person called antidiabetic agents. Based on mechanism medicines classified into insulinotropic and non-insulinotropic, similarly, monotherapy and combination are available. A study by Daniel *et al.* (2014) isolated marine Actinomycetes using Starch Caesin Agar medium (SCNA) from the Bay of Bengal, an unexploited ecosystem; the metabolites from the strains were extracted after culturing in ISP2 (Yeast Extract Malt Extract agar) medium for assessing antidiabetic activities and they reported a strain JKC-M1 was highly potent. Endophytic actinobacteria, a total of 65 numbers were isolated from *Tinospora crispa, Caesalpinia sappans* and *Curcuma aeruginosa* respectively. Out of several strains, 12 were reported with antidiabetic property and the BWA65 strain was more effective in antidiabetic metabolite production than others strains. (Golinska *et al.*, 2015). Voglibose, Acarbose, valienamine, adiposin-1, and trestatin-B were reported from *Streptomyces hygroscopicus-limoneus, S. calvus* and *S.*

dimorphogenes, and these are used as antidiabetic agents. These compounds are reported for treating type-2 diabetes, voglibose is an alpha-glucosidase inhibitor that lowers the blood glucose levels (Alharbi, 2016).

Pujiyanto *et al.* (2012) reported a group of endophytic actinobacteria with the antidiabetic property. *Tinospora crispa, Caesalpinia sappans and Curcuma aeruginosa* were selected for the isolation and 12 out of 65 reported with antidiabetic property. *Streptomyces olivochromogenes* isolated from *Tinospora crisp* reported as bioactive strain with antidiabetic metabolite production. *Streptomyces longisporoflavus* and *Streptomyces* sp. were isolated from *Leucas ciliate* and *Rauwolfia densiflora* with antidiabetic property (Akshatha *et al.* 2014). Alpha-Amylase inhibiting metabolite was discovered from marine actinobacteria. Samples were collected from coastal areas of Kothapattanam, Ongole, Andhra Pradesh; a total of 20 actinobacteria were isolated and VITMA1 was selected as bioactive strain and the strain identified up to genus level *as Streptomyces* sp. (Elizabeth Mathew *et al.*, 2017). Soil samples were collected from Kaas Plateau and Tamhini Ghat, Maharashtra, and serial diluted on Starch Casein Agar (SCA) medium for isolation; from the pure culture, silver nanoparticles were synthesized using 1 mM silver nitrate ($AgNO_3$). The synthesized siver nanoparticles were analyzed using UV-Vis spectroscopy, SEM analysis, and FTIR analysis; these particles were further confirmed to possess anti-diabetic property (Rajashree *et al.*, 2015).

7. Antiinflammatory agents from Actinobacteria

Anti-inflammatory drugs are used to reduce stress, pain, and body temperature. These agents will block the function of Cyclooxygenase (or COX) enzyme which responsible for the production of prostaglandins and will reduce body discomforts. The bioactive strain *Streptomyces* sp. SUC1 was isolated from aerial roots of *Ficus benjamina* collected from Silpakorn University, Nakorn Pathom, Thailand. Different morphological characters including aerial and substrate mycelium colour, spore morphology, and diffusible pigment production was recorded using Yeast Malt Extract Medium (ISP2). Later metabolite extraction was carried out using different organic solvents. UV spectroscopy, C and H NMR, Electron ionization mass spectra (EIMS), TLC, preparative laser chromatography (PLC) were performed for the profiling of metabolites. Anti-inflammatory activity was studied by using RAW 264.7 cell which maintained at Dulbecco's Modified Eagle Medium (DMEM) supplemented with 10 % heat-inactivated fetal bovine serum (FBS), penicillin G (100 IU/ml), streptomycin (100 mg/ml), and L-glutamine (2 mM) and incubated at 37°C in a humidified atmosphere containing 5 % CO2. The compound lansai C inhibit the production of various immune components includes nitric oxide (NO), prostaglandin

E2 (PGE2), tumor necrosis factor (TNF-a), interleukin (IL)-1a, IL-6, and IL-10, but also on inducible NO synthase and cyclooxygenase-2 (COX-2) (Taechowisan *et al.*, 2009).

Girao (2019) reported anti-inflammatory compound producing actinobacteria isolated from macroalgae. Marine sediment samples were collected from kottakodduru of Nellore district, Andhra Pradesh used for marine actinobacteria isolation. A total of 15 isolates were observed on Starch Casein Agar, Nutrient Glucose Agar, and Maltose Yeast Extract agar. The strain (KN8) was selected as a bioactive strain with anti-inflammatory metabolite production. Anti-inflammatory activity by red blood cells membrane stabilization was studied with ethyl acetate extract showed 33 % of protection at a concentration of 400 μg/ml (Lavanyalatha *et al.*, 2014). *Streptomyces violaceoruber* isolated from *Equus burchelli* feces reported with anti-inflammatory property. Three new metabolites with one reported metabolite namely GTRI-02 were discovered from the bioactive strain and further the characterization was done by using different methods includes NMR spectroscopic data analysis as well as UV, IR, and MS data. One compound was reported with inhibition of nitric oxide (NO) production in lipopolysaccharide (LPS)-stimulated and another compound was observed with moderate inhibition of NO production (Ma *et al.*, 2017).

Streptomyces gramineus, a bioactive strain with anti-inflammatory activity was isolated from *Leptogium trichophorum*. Six new metabolites namely actinofuranones D-I (compounds 1–6) and known compounds JBIR-108 (7), E-975 (8), and E-492 (9) were derived. Compounds 4, 5, 8, and 9 were reported with nitric oxide (NO) production suppression due to the suppression of the activity of nitric oxide synthase (iNOS). NMR spectroscopic details, UV, IR, and MS data were used for the profiling of metabolites. It was observed that compounds 4, 5, 8, and 9 inhibited LPS-induced release of proinflammatory cytokines interleukin-6 (IL-6) and tumor necrosis factor (TNF) (Jian Ma *et al.*, 2018).

8. Anticancer or Antitumor agents from Actinobacteria

Food and Drug Administration US approved 150 numbers of anticancer drugs and broadly classified them into two groups which include 61 cytotoxic-based drugs and 89 target-based drugs. Cytotoxic drugs will kill rapidly dividing cells by targeting on DNA or mitochondria and block replication. The second group will interact at the molecular level and avoid the spreading and growth of cells. From mangrove soil samples, three different actinobacteria strains were isolated namely *Microbacterium mangrove* MUSC 115T, *Sinomonas humi* MUSC 117T and *Monashia flava* MUSC 78T. The metabolites produced by these strains were checked for its anticancer activity using two different cell lines namely human colon cancer cell lines (HT-29) and human cervical carcinoma cell lines (Ca Ski) followed by MTT assay. From the results, it has been recorded that *M. mangrovi* MUSC 115T and *M. flava* MUSC 78T exhibited anticancer effects against Ca Ski cell line (Azman *et al.*, 2017). Chen *et al.*, (2018) screened metabolite of *Streptomyces nigra sp. nov.* isolated from rhizosphere soil of mangrove region for its anticancer activity using various cancer cell lines including A549, HCT-116, and HepG2. Employing gas chromatography Mass Spectroscopy (GC)-MS and liquid chromatography Mass Spectroscopy (LC)-MS analysis, 16 types of metabolites were identified, these were found to have anticancer activities; 3 compounds were found to be more efficient and analysed further. Observed details summarized that cyclo(Pro-Ala) and cyclo (Pro-Met) against A549 cells, cyclo (Phe-Pro) and cyclo (Pro-Ala) against HCT-116 cells are better in activity.

Sample collected from Brazil used for actinobacteria isolation and anticancer activity was assessed for its metabolites. A total of 94 strains were isolated for screening using HCT-116 cell line and 224 extracts used for the same among this 41 were significantly effective against cancer cell. Profiling of active compounds using different methods identified piericidins A and C, glucopiericidin, and three known diketopiperazines, cyclo (Phe-*trans*-4-OH-Pro), cyclo (L Phe-L-Pro), and cyclo (L-Trp-L-Pro) compounds from the metabolites are responsible for the same property (Ferreira *et al.*, 2016). *Streptomyces* sp. MUM256 isolated from Malaysia soil subjected for anticancer activity study. Eight different cancer cells were used and most sensitive against HCT116 followed by HT29, and Caco-2 respectively. Phenolic and pyrrolopyrazine were profiled using Gas Chromatography and Mass Spectroscopy (GC-MS) (Tan *et al.*, 2015).

Actinobacteria isolated from Antarctica was reported for anticancer activity (Leonardo Jose Silva *et al.*, 2020). A total of 72 isolates were recorded; amongst, *Streptomyces* sp. CMAA 1527 and *Streptomyces* sp. CMAA 1653 were selected as bioactive strains with cinerubin B and actinomycin V as active metabolites. Breast (MCF-7), glioblastoma (U251), lung/non-small (NCI-H460), and kidney (786-0) were selected for anticancer activity study using these metabolites. In another study, *Streptomyces avidinii* strain SU4 isolated from marine region and are reported for anticancer metabolite production. The anticancer assay results revealed that 64.5 µg for Hep-2 cell lines and 250 µg for VERO cell lines. Phthalate 1,2-benzene dicarboxylic acid, bis(2-methylpropyl) ester (12.17 %), isooctyl phthalate (15.29 %) were reported are the active compounds (Sudha and Masila Maniselvam, 2012).

9. Conclusion and Perspectives

Use of natural agents for medicinal applications dated back from stone age onwards. Better efficacy and less side effects are the most valuable qualities of these agents. Actinobacteria is a potential reported microbial population with wide range of species. Commercially available 80 % of microbial products are reported from actinobacteria and predominately from *Streptomyces* sp. due to high G+C, content in the cell. Bioprospecting of metabolites from microbial based sources are the current scenario of biology. The aforementioned details concluded that the wide applications of molecules in pharmacological field and the notable property is, single molecule can use for multiple applications from a single species.

10. References

1) Abd-Elnaby, H. Abo-Elala, G. Abdel-Raouf, U. Abd-elwahab, A. and Hamed, M. (2016). Antibacterial and anticancer activity of marine *Streptomyces parvus*: optimization and application. *Biotechnology and Biotechnological Equipment*, 30(1): 180-191.
2) Abraham, J. and Chauhan, R. (2018). Profiling of red pigment produced by *Streptomyces* sp. JAR6 and its bioactivity. *Biotechnology*, 8(1): 1 - 9.
3) Abreu, C. Rocha-Pereira, N. Sarmento, A. and Magro, F. 2015. *Nocardia* infections among immunomodulated inflammatory bowel disease patients: a review. *World Journal of Gastroenterology*, 21: 6491 – 6498.
4) Adam, D. Maciejewska, M. Naômé, A. Martinet, L. Coppieters, W. Karim, L. and Rigali, S. (2018). Isolation, characterization, and antibacterial activity of hard-to-culture actinobacteria from cave moonmilk deposits. *Antibiotics*, 7(2): 28.
5) Akshatha, V. J. Nalini, M. S. D'souza, C. and Prakash, H. S. (2014). Streptomycete endophytes from anti-diabetic medicinal plants of the Western Ghats inhibit alpha-amylase and promote glucose uptake. *Letters in Applied Microbiology*, 58(5): 433-439.
6) Alharbi, N. S. (2016). Novel bioactive molecules from marine actinomycetes. *Biosciences Biotechnology Research Asia*, 13(4): 1905-1927.
7) Araujo, J.M.D. Silva, A.C.D and Azevedo, J. L. 2000. Isolation of endophytic actinomycetes from roots and leaves of maize (*Zea mays* L.). *Brazilian Arches of Biology and Technology*, 43(4): 447 – 451.
8) Ayswaria, R. Vasu, V and Krishna, R. 2020. Diverse endophytic Streptomyces species with dynamic metabolites and their meritorious applications: a critical review. *Critical Reviews in Microbiology*, 46(6): 750 - 758.

9) Azimi, S. Baserisalehi, M. and Bahador, N. (2014). Evaluation of antimicrobial pigment produced by Streptomyces coeruleorubidus. *Nature Environment and Pollution Technology*, 13(3): 641 - 644.

10) Azman, A. S. Othman, I. Fang, C. M. Chan, K. G. Goh, B. H. and Lee, L. H. (2017). Antibacterial, anticancer and neuroprotective activities of rare Actinobacteria from mangrove forest soils. *Indian Journal of Microbiology*, 57(2): 177-187.

11) Bell, K.S. Philp. J.C. Aw, D.W and Christofi. N. 1998. The genus *Rhodococcus*. *Journal of Applied Microbiology*, 85: 195 – 210.

12) Benndorf, R. Guo, H. Sommerwerk, E. Weigel, C. Garcia-Altares, M. Martin, K. and Beemelmanns, C. (2018). Natural products from Actinobacteria associated with fungus-growing termites. *Antibiotics*, 7(3): 83 - 89.

13) Bentley, S.D. Maiwald, M. Murphy, L.D. Pallen, M.J. Yeats, C.A. Dover, L.G. Norbertczak, H.T. Besra, G.S. Quail, M.A. Harris, D.E. von Herbay, A.Goble, A. Rutter, S. Squares, R. Squares, S. Barrell, B.G. Parkhill, J. and Relman, D.A. 2003. Sequencing and analysis of the genome of the Whipple's disease bacterium *Tropheryma whipplei*. *Lancet*, 361: 637 – 644.

14) Bhosale, R. S. Hajare, K. Y. Mulay, B. Mujumdar, S., and Kothawade, M. (2015). Biosynthesis, characterization and study of antimicrobial effect of silver nanoparticles by *Actinomycetes* spp. *International Journal of Current Microbiology and Applied Sciences*, 2: 144 - 151.

15) Bose, U. Hewavitharana, A. K. Vidgen, M. E. Ng, Y.K. Shaw, P. N. Fuerst, J.A. and Hodson, M. P. 2014. Discovering the recondite secondary metabolome spectrum of *Salinispora* species: a study of inter-species diversity. *PLoS One*, 12: 155 - 164.

16) Castillo, U.F. Strobel, G.A. Ford, E.J. Hess, W.M. Porter, H. Jensen, J.B. Albert, H. Robison, R. Condron, M.A.M. and Teplow, D.B. 2002. Munumbicins, wide-spectrum antibiotics produced by Streptomyces NRRL 30562, endophytic on *Kennedia nigriscans*. *Microbiology (Reading)*, 148(Pt 9): 2675 – 26850

17) Chen, C. Ye, Y. Wang, R. Zhang, Y. Wu, C. Debnath, S. C. and Wu, M. (2018). *Streptomyces nigra* is a novel actinobacterium isolated from mangrove soil and exerts a potent antitumor activity *in vitro*. *Frontiers in Microbiology*, 9: 1587.

18) Collins, M.D. 1994. Isoprenoid quinones, In Goodfellow M, O'Donnell AG (ed), Chemical methods in prokaryotic systematics. Wiley, Chichester, United Kingdom, 265–309.

19) Collins, M.D. Goodfellow, M. Minnikin, D.E. Alderson, G. 1985. Menaquinone composition of mycolic acid-containing actinomycetes and some *Sporoactinomycetes*. *Journal of Applied Bacteriology*, 58: 77 - 86.
20) Daniel, K., Guravaiah, M., Rama Lakshmi, K., Revathi, T., Usha Rani, K., Nirosha, P and Siva Kumar, S. (2014). Screening, Isolation and Production of Bioactive Compounds from Marine Actinomycetes. *Journal of Marine Science*, 3(3): 201 - 214.
21) Dastager, S., Dayanand, L.W.J.A., Tang, S. K., Tian, X. P., Zhi, X. Y., Xu, L.H and Jiang C. 2006. Separation, identification and analysis of pigment (melanin) production in *Streptomyces*. *African Journal of Biotechnology*, 5: 1131 – 1134.
22) de Moura, P. A., de Albuquerque Lima, T. Ferreira, M. R. A. Soares, L. A. L., de Souza Lima, G. M. Napoleão, T. H. and Paiva, P. M. G. (2021). The relevance of actinobacteria as sources of antioxidant compounds: Evaluation of *Streptomyces* isolates from rhizosphere collected at Brazilian Caatinga. In *Microbial and Natural Macromolecules* (401 - 418). Academic Press.
23) Desnues, B. A., Moussawi, K. and Fenollar, F. 2010. New insights into Whipple's disease and *Tropheryma whipplei* infections. *Microbes Infections*, 12: 1102 – 1110.
24) Dietz, A. and Mathews, J. 1971. Classification of *Streptomyces* spore surfaces into five groups. *Applied Microbiology*, 21: 527 – 533.
25) Elizabeth Mathew, Haimanti Mondal, Priyanka Kharat, Purbasha Saha and Bhaskara Rao. *In-Vitro* Alpha-Amylase Inhibitor Activity and Antioxidant Activity of Actinobacteria isolated from Marine Sediment samples. *Journal of Marine Sciences*, 9(3): 64 - 70.
26) Ezra, D., Castillo, U. F., Strobel, G. A., Hess, W. M., Porter, H., Jensen, J. B., Condron, M. A. M., Teplow, D. B., Sears, J and Maranta, M. (2004). Coronamycins, peptide antibiotics produced by a verticillate *Streptomyces* sp. (MSU-2110) endophytic on *Monstera* sp. *Microbiology Society*, 150(4): 785 – 793.
27) Ferreira, E. G, Torres, M. D. C. M. da Silva, A. B. Colares, L. L. Pires, K. Lotufo, T. M. and Jimenez, P. C. (2016). Prospecting Anticancer Compounds in Actinomycetes Recovered from the Sediments of Saint Peter and Saint Paul's Archipelago, Brazil. *Chemistry and Biodiversity*, 13(9): 1149 - 1157.
28) Flärdh, K and Buttner, M. J. (2009). *Streptomyces* morphogenetics: dissecting differentiation in a filamentous bacterium. *Nature Reviews Microbiology*, 7: 36 – 49.

29) Gao, B and Gupta, R. S. 2012. Phylogenetic framework and molecular signatures for the main clades of the phylum Actinobacteria. *Microbiology and Molecular Biology Reviews*, 76: 66 – 112.

30) Girão, M. Ribeiro, I. Ribeiro, T. Azevedo, I. C. Pereira, F. Urbatzka, R and Carvalho, M. F. (2019). Actinobacteria isolated from *Laminaria ochroleuca*: a source of new bioactive compounds. *Frontiers in Microbiology*, 10: 683 - 690.

31) Golinska, P., Wypij, M., Agarkar, G., Rathod, D., Dahm, H and Rai, M. (2015). Endophytic actinobacteria of medicinal plants: diversity and bioactivity. *Antonie Van Leeuwenhoek*, 108(2): 267 - 289.

32) Goodfellow, M. O and Donnell, A. G. (1989). Search and discovery of industrially-significant actinomycetes, p 343–383. In Baumberg S, Hunter IS, Rhodes PM (ed), Microbial products: new approach. Cambridge University Press, Cambridge, United Kingdom.

33) Gozari, M. Bahador, N. Jassbi, A. R. Mortazavi, M. S. and Eftekhar, E. (2018). Antioxidant and cytotoxic activities of metabolites produced by a new marine *Streptomyces* sp. isolated from the sea cucumber *Holothuria leucospilota*. *Iranian Journal of Fisheries Sciences*, 17(2): 413 - 426.

34) Hirsch, A. M and Valdés, M. (2009). *Micromonospora*: an important microbe for biomedicine and potentially for biocontrol and biofuels. *Soil Biology and Biochemistry*, 42: 536 – 542.

35) Igarashi, Y. 2004. Screening of novel bioactive compounds from plant-associated actinomycetes. *Actinomycetologica*, 18(2): 63 - 66.

36) Jacobson, R. R and Krahenbuhl, J. L. 1999. Leprosy. *Lancet*, 353: 655 – 660.

37) Janardhan, A. Kumar, A. P. Viswanath, B. Saigopal, D. V. R and Narasimha, G. (2014). Production of bioactive compounds by actinomycetes and their antioxidant properties. *Biotechnology Research International*, 20: 14 - 22.

38) Janssen, P. H., Yates, P. S., Grinton, B. E., Taylor, P. M and Sait, M. 2002. Improved culturability of soil bacteria and isolation in pure culture of novel members of the divisions *Acidobacteria*, *Actinobacteria*, *Proteobacteria* and *Verrucomicrobia*. *Applied and Environmental Microbiology*, 68: 2391 - 2396.

39) Jessy Padma, B. Saraswathi, K. Arumugam, P and Anna Shiny, R. 2018. Isolation, characterization and evaluation of antioxidant activities of secondary metabolites producing actinomycetes of terrestrial origin. *International Journal of Research in Medical Sciences*, 6(3): 1017 - 1028.

40) Kamarudheen, N., Naushad, T. and Rao, K. V. B. 2019. Biosynthesis, Characterization and Antagonistic Applications of Extracellular Melanin Pigment from Marine *Nocardiopsis* sp. *Indian Journal of Pharmaceutical Education and Research*, 53: 112 - 120.

41) Kim, S. B. Lonsdale, J. Seong, C. N and Goodfellow, M. 2003. *Streptacidiphilus* gen. nov., acidophilic actinomycetes with wall chemotype I and emendation of the family Streptomycetaceae.
42) Kim, T. K., Thomas, S. M., Ho, M., Sharma, S., Reich, C. I., Frank, J. A., Yeater, K. M., Biggs, D. R. Nakamura, N and Stumpf, R. 2009. Heterogeneity of vaginal microbial communities within individuals. *Journal of Clinical Microbiology*, 47: 1181 - 1189.
43) Kroppenstedt, R. 1985. Fatty acid and menaquinone analysis of actinomycetes and related organisms, Chemical methods in bacterial systematics. SAB Technical Series 20, Academic Press, London, United Kingdom, 173 – 199.
44) Labeda, D. 1987. Actinomycete taxonomy: generic characterization. *Developments in Industrial Microbiology*, 28: 115 - 121.
45) Lavanyalatha, Y., Rashmi, H. K and Uma Maheswari Devi, P. 2014. *In vitro* Antioxidant and Antiinflammatory Potential of Marine Actinomycetes. *Journal of Marine Science*, 5(12): 201 - 204
46) Lechevalier, H. A and Lechevalier, M. P. 1965. Classification des actinomycètes aérobies basée sur leur morphologie composition chimique. *Annales de Institut Pasteur*, 108: 662 – 673.
47) Lechevalier, M. P and Lechevalier, H. 1970. Chemical composition as a criterion in the classification of aerobic Actinomycetes. *International Journal of Bacteriology*, 20: 435 - 443.
48) Leuchtenberger, W., Huthmacher, K and Drauz, K. 2005. Biotechnological production of amino acids and derivatives: current status and prospects. *Applied Microbiology and Biotechnology*, 69: 1 – 8.
49) Ludwig, W. Euzéby, J. Schumann, P. Buss. H.J. Trujillo, M.E. Kämpfer, P. and Whiteman, W.B. (2012). Road map of the phylum Actinobacteria, 1–28.
50) Ma, J. Cao, B. Liu, C. Guan, P. Mu, Y. Jiang, Y. and Huang, X. 2018. Actinofuranones DI from a lichen-associated actinomycetes, *Streptomyces gramineus*, and their anti-inflammatory effects. *Molecules*, *23*(9): 2393.
51) Ma, J., Lei, H., Chen, X., Bi, X., Jiang, Y., Han, L and Huang, X. 2017. New anti-inflammatory metabolites produced by *Streptomyces violaceoruber* isolated from Equus burchelli feces. *The Journal of Antibiotics*, 70(10): 991 - 994.
52) Manivasagan, P., Venkatesan, J., Sivakumar, K and Kim, S. K. (2013). Marine actinobacterial metabolites: current status and future perspectives. *Microbiological Research*, 168: 311 – 332.

53) Mohammadipanah, F and Momenilandi, M. (2018). Potential of rare actinomycetes in the production of metabolites against multiple oxidant agents. *Pharmaceutical Biology*, 56(1): 51 - 59.

54) Nagaseshu, P., Gayatridevi, V., Kumar, A. B., Kumari, S., Mohan, M. G and Malla, R. 2016. Antioxidant and antiproliferative potentials of marine actinomycetes. *International Journal of Pharmacy and Pharmaceutical. Sciences,* 8: 277 - 284.

55) Orla Jensen S. 1924. La classification des bactéries lactiques. *Lait,* 4: 468 – 474.

56) Parmar, R. S and Singh, C. 2018. A comprehensive study of eco-friendly natural pigment and its applications. *Biochemistry and Biophysics Reports*, 13: 22 - 26.

57) Passari, A. K., Mishra, V. K., Singh, G., Singh, P., Kumar, B., Gupta, V. K., Sarma, R. K., Saikia, R., Donovan, A. O and Singh, B. P. 2017. Insights into the functionality of endophytic actinobacteria with a focus on their biosynthetic potential and secondary metabolites production. *Scientific Reports*, 7(1): 1 - 17

58) Praptiwi, D., Fathoni, A. Putri, A. L., Wulansari, D and Agusta, A. (2019). Assessment of actinomycetes isolated from soils on Simeuleu Island as antibacterial and antioxidant. In *AIP Conference Proceedings*, 2120 (1):080011). AIP Publishing LLC.

59) Pridham, T. G., Hesseltine, C. W and Benedict, R. G. (1958). A guide for the classification of *Streptomyces* according to selected groups; placement of strains in morphological sections. *Applied Microbiology*, 6: 52 - 79.

60) Pujiyanto, S., Lestari, Y. U. L. I. N., Suwanto, A., Budiarti, S and Darusman, L. K. (2012). Alpha-glucosidase inhibitor activity and characterization of endophytic actinomycetes isolated from some Indonesian diabetic medicinal plants. *International Journal of Pharmacy and Pharmaceutical Sciences*, 4(1): 327 - 333.

61) Roy, S and Banerjee, D. 2015. Bioactive endophytic actinomycetes of *Cinnamomum* sp.; isolation, identification, activity guided purification and process optimization of active metabolite. *American Journal of Microbiology and Antimicrobials*, 6(1): 4 - 13.

62) Savi, D. C., Haminiuk, C. W. I., Sora, G. T. S., Adamoski, D. M., Kenski, J., Winnischofer, S. M. B and Glienke, C. 2015. Antitumor, antioxidant and antibacterial activities of secondary metabolites extracted by endophytic actinomycetes isolated from *Vochysia divergens*. *International Journal of Pharmaceutical, Chemical and Biological Sciences*, 5(1): 1111 - 1120.

63) Shivlata, L and Satyanarayana, T. 2017. Actinobacteria in agricultural and environmental sustainability. *Agro-environmental Sustainability,* 10: 173 - 218.
64) Siddharth, S and Vittal, R. R. 2018. Evaluation of antimicrobial, enzyme inhibitory, antioxidant and cytotoxic activities of partially purified volatile metabolites of marine *Streptomyces* sp. S2A. *Microorganisms*, 6(3): 72 - 75.
65) Silva, L. J., Crevelin, E. J., Souza, D. T., Lacerda-Júnior, G. V., de Oliveira, V. M., Ruiz, A. L and Melo, I. S. 2020. Actinobacteria from Antarctica as a source for anticancer discovery. *Scientific Reports*, 10(1): 1 - 15.
66) Soundari, A. P. G., Mani, V. M. Bose, V. S. C. Jabastin, J and Priyadarisini, V. B. 2017. A Preliminary Assessment of Yellow Pigment from *Streptomyces parvulus* C5-5Y. *Journal of Pure and Applied Microbiology*, 11(1): 197 - 203.
67) Soundari, P. G. A. Mani, M. Karthiyaini, D. Priyadharshini, U. Jeeva, S and Priyadarisini, B. 2017. Bioprospecting fungicidal metabolite producing marine actinomycetes from southern coastal regions of India. *International Journal of Life Science and Pharma Research*, 7(4): L55 - L64.
68) Srinivasan, M., Keziah, S. M., Hemalatha, M and Devi, C. S. 2017. Pigment from *Streptomyces bellus* MSA1 isolated from marine sediments. *IOP Conference Series: Materials Science and Engineering,* 263(2): 022049.
69) Subramanian, D., Kim, M. S., Kim, D. H and Heo, M. S. 2017. Isolation, characterization, antioxidant, antimicrobial and cytotoxic effect of marine Actinomycete, *Streptomyces carpaticus* MK-01, against fish pathogens. *Brazilian Archives of Biology and Technology*, 60: 2530 - 2542.
70) Suzuki, K. Goodfellow, M and O'Donnell, A, G. 1993. Cell envelopes and classification, In Handbook of new bacterial systematics. Academic Press, London, United Kingdom. 195 – 250.
71) Swarnalakshmi, K., Senthilkumar, M and Ramakrishnan, B. 2016. Endophytic actinobacteria: nitrogen fixation, phytohormone production, and antibiosis. In Plant growth promoting actinobacteria, 123-145.
72) Taechowisan, T and Lumyong, S. 2003. Activity of endophytic actimomycetes from roots of *Zingiber officinale* and *Alpinia galanga* against phytopathogenic fungi. *Annals of Microbiology*, 53(3): 291 – 298.
73) Taechowisan, T., Wanbanjob, A., Tuntiwachwuttikul, P and Liu, J. 2009. Anti-inflammatory activity of lansais from endophytic *Streptomyces* sp. SUC1 in LPS-induced RAW 264.7 cells. *Food and Agricultural Immunology*, 20(1): 67 - 77.
74) Tan, L. T. H., Ser, H. L., Yin, W. F., Chan, K. G., Lee, L. H and Goh, B. H. 2015. Investigation of antioxidative and anticancer potentials of Streptomyces sp. MUM256 isolated from Malaysia mangrove soil. *Frontiers in Microbiology*, 6: 1316.

75) Tsukamura, M. 1971. Proposal of a new genus, Gordona, for slightly acid-fast organisms occurring in sputa of patients with pulmonary disease and in soil. *Journal of General Microbiology*, 68: 15 – 26.

76) Udhyakumar, K., Ramalingam, S., Saravanan, R and Dheeba, B. 2017. Extraction of Actinomycetes (*Streptomyces* sp.) pigment and evaluation of its anticancer propertyon HeLa cell line. *Der Pharma Chemica*, 9(24): 106 - 113.

77) Usha, R and Kingsley, B. A. (2018). *Streptomyces* sp. – A promising source of antimicrobial agent. *Journal of Analytical and Pharmaceutical Research*, 7(3): 323 - 328.

78) Van Dissel, D., Claessen, D and Van Wezel G. P. (2014). Morphogenesis of Streptomyces in submerged cultures. *Advances in Applied Microbiology*, 89: 1 - 45.

79) Ventura, M., Canchaya, C., Fitzgerald, G. F., Gupta, R. S and van Sinderen, D. 2007. Genomics as a means to understand bacterial phylogeny and ecological adaptation: the case of *Bifidobacteria*. *Antonie Van Leeuwenhoek*, 91: 351 – 372.

80) Williams, S. T., Goodfellow, M and Alderson, G. 1989. Genus *Streptomyces* Waksman and Henrici 1943, 339AL, 2452–2492.

Advances in Pharmaceutical Sciences
ISBN: 978-81-951323-7-9
First Edition; Volume – 1; 2021
Chapter – 4, Page: 38 - 45

4

PHARMACEUTICAL COMPONENTS FROM MARINE FLORA AND FAUNA

J. Albino Wins[1] and M. Murugan[2*]

[1]Department of Botany, Holy Cross College (Autonomous), Nagercoil – 4, Kanyakumari District, Tamil Nadu.
[2]Department of Biomedical Sciences, Noorul Islam Centre for Higher Education, Kumaracoil, Kanyakumari District, Tami lNadu.

E.mail: winsbt@gmail.com

Abstract

Therapeutically important compounds of present scenario can be extracted from diversified natural sources like plants, animals, marine organisms, and microorganisms. Marine biota accounts for about 50 % of the world biodiversity, but their active potential as a rich source of novel bioactive compounds and their applications towards pharmaceutical and nutraceutical industries have grown recently. Marine microflora and fauna like Algae, Sponges, Bacteria, Fungi, Actinomycetes and Corals possess many bioactive substances, and can be used in the treatment of cancer, anemia, diarrhea, obesity, diabetes, atopic dermatitis etc. The most implemented natural products of marine are mainly accumulated in the invertebrates such as sponges, tunicates, bryozoans, and mollusks. They are a great highlight for natural antioxidants, colours, immunosuppressants, enzyme inhibitors, hypocholesterolemic agents, vitamins, enzymes, and antibiotics. Apart from these, they possess special concern towards food ingredients and dietary supplements, which is the special need of all human beings.

Key words: Therapeutic importance, Natural products, Bioactive compounds, Human health, Marine flora and fauna.

1. Introduction

People have relied upon nature for their straightforward necessities just like the hotspots for prescriptions, covers, food stuffs, scents, clothing, flavors, manures and methods for transportation all through the ages. For the huge extents of total populace restorative plants keep on showing a prevailing job in the medical care framework and this is essentially evident in non-industrial nations, where natural medication has persistent history of long use. The turn of events and acknowledgment of restorative and monetary guides of these plants are on ascent in both industrialized and agricultural countries. Nature has abundance source of pharmaceutical products that is traditionally used by us. Today, more than 50 % of the pharmaceutical medicines and drugs are extracted and prepared from the natural resources or synthesizedby the usage of natural products as a starting material. Since ancient times, early people soley used natural medicines, in the form of crude extracts from plants, to treat infection, inflammation, pain, and other maladies (National Academies Press, 1999). Even today, in many parts of the world, natural medicines are considered as the only treatments for treating all their health ailments.

Approximately, 70 % of our planet's surface is covered by oceans. The representatives of the entire phylum are found in the sea, and among that, twelve phyla are exclusively marine. Marine biodiversity makes a potential and maximal source of different varieties of novel bioactive compounds (Delaney, 1985). These compounds are mostly synthesized as secondary metabolites, by the marine microflora and fauna. Actually, large number of potential bioactive compounds is found in the oceans as well as deep sea with efficient biological properties and pharmaceutical efficacies. These active ingredients have a great impact on a wide application of treating malignancy, anemic disorders, dysentery and diarrhea, obesity, diabetes, dermatitis, infections, inflammations, etc. (Anderson, 1995).

The marine environment has adopted a great focus on natural products drug discovery research because of its relatively unexplored biodiversity. The natural pharmaceutical efficacy products of marine are mainly seen in most of the invertebrate organisms like sponges, tunicates, bryozoans, and mollusks. Approximately, more than 2400 natural products have been isolated from macroalgae (Gai *et al.*, 2007).

Seaweeds have a remarkable potency against diabetes, microbial infections, and inflammations because they are a great reservoir of many chemical constituents like acids, alkaloids, amines, antibacterial substances, antifungal substances, antiviral substances, lipids, sterols, steroids, fatty acids, phenolic compounds, phytochromes, pigments, proteins, peptides, amino acids, sugar, alcohols, and vitamins.

Gracilaria opuntia belongs to the family Rhodophyceae (Red algae) and possesses various biological activities with pharmaceutical effects. The marine flora includes a wide range of organisms from sponges, tunicates, bryozoans, mollusks to bacteria, microalgae, macroalgae, and cyanobacteria. The bioactive metabolites produced due to their metabolic activity are effective in treating numerous infectious and non-infectious diseases. Marine microflora including algae are widely used in the development of various nutraceuticals and are also used as food source or food ingredients (Xiong *et al.*, 2009). Algae include both the micro- and macroforms and both the types are used as nutraceuticals.

2. Prokaryotic Organisms

The prokaryotic communities were mostly found in the organic rich deep marine sediments, which are mostly associated with methane hydrates. The marine bacteria and fungi are now a great target of biomedical studies, in developing novel medicines for incurable diseases.

Marine Bacteria

Marine bacteria thrive in harsh oceanic climates and are the constant producers of valuable secondary metabolites. The marine bacteria *Pseudomonas* is a Gram negative, γ-proteo-bacteria harboring with more bioactive compounds. The bacterium strain KMM 3042 is aerobic, non-pigmented and can produce bioactive components like pyrroles, pseudopeptide pyrrolidinedione, phloroglucinol, phenazine, benzaldehyde, quinoline, quinolone, phenanthren, phthalate, andrimid, moiramides, zafrin, and bushrin. *Stenotrophomonas* bacterial strains isolated from the sponges and sea urchins, showed antibacterial and antifungal properties. They are also active against the fungal strain *Candida albicans* and can inhibit the Gram-positive microorganisms (Chapman *et al.,* 2015). *Stenotrophomonas maltophilia* is an opportunistic pathogen that possesses biocontrolling capabilities.

The marine ark shell *Anadara broughtoni* with the associated heterotrophic bacteria also possess antimicrobial and hemolytic properties. *Pseudoalteromonas*, can inhibit methicillin-resistant *Staphylococcus aureus* (MRSA), due to the presence of a brominated biphenyl compound, 3,3″,5,5″-tetrabromo2,2″-diphenyldiol. It also exhibits antifungal properties. The *Pseudoalteromonas luteoviolacea* has the tendency to inhibit the protists (Li *et al.*, 2006).

Marine Fungi

Marine fungi produce a wide variety of bioactive metabolites that possess anticancer, antibacterial, antiplasmodial, anti-inflammatory, and antiviral activity. An anthraquinone derivative with naphtho [1,2,3-de]chromene-2,7-dione skeleton was isolated from *Aspergillus glaucus*. It possess cytotoxicity against K562 and P388 cell lines. Similarly, *Penicillium* sp., was also found to exhibit antitumor activities. The fungi *Ampelomyces* sp. possesses potent antimicrobial and antifouling compounds. It has antilarvicidal effect because of 3-chloro2,5-dihydroxybenzyl alcohol, that effectively inhibit the larva *Hydroides elegans* and *Balanus amphitrite* (Winston, 1988).

Cladosporium sp. also exhibit antibiotic and antifouling activity. *Fusarium* sp. possess novel antimitotic and antifungal activity, because of the chemical compound Fusarielin E. *Pseudallescheria* produce different components like dioxopiperazine, dihydroxy bisdethiobis and methylthiogliotoxin, that exhibit antibacterial activity against multidrug-resistant bacteria. Exophiala exhibit a mild antibacterial activity against *Staphylococcus aureus* due to Chlorohydroaspyrones A and B. *Lachnum papyraceum* possess nematicidal effect. *Phomaherbarum* has radical scavenging activity against DPPH due to halogenated benzoquinones (Inagaki *et al.*, 2006).

Marine Actinomycetes

Actinomycetes are the great producers of secondary metabolites. Many antibiotics like Penicillin, Streptomycin, Erythromycin, and Tetracycline, are produced byactinomycetes. Apart from that, they are producers of novel antitumor, antimalarial, and antimicrobial compounds.

Nocardiopsis lucentensis produced different chemical constituents like Lucentamycins A, B, C and D. Lucentamycins A and B has cytotoxic effect against human colon carcinoma. *Streptomyces* sp. produce Mansouramycin A, B, C and D, that exhibit cytotoxic effect against lung cancer, breast cancer, melanoma, and prostate cancer drugs (Trischman *et al.,* 1994).

Macrodiolide Tartrolon D from *Streptomyces* sp. has strong cytotoxic activity against lung, colon and breast tumor cell lines. *Saccharomonospora* sp. produce an alkaloid Lodopyridone that is cytotoxic to human colon cancer cells. *Marinispora* has bisindolepyrroles and Lynamicins A–E, that exhibit antimicrobial activity against both Gram-positive and Gram-negative bacteria, methicillin resistant *Staphylococcus aureus* (MRSA) and vancomycin-resistant bacteria. The dienoyltetramic acids tirandamycin C and D compound isolated from *Streptomyces* sp, which is effective against vancomycin-resistant *Enterococcus faecalis*. *Streptomyces* sp. isolate has

Trioxacarcins A, B, and C with good antimicrobial, antitumor, and antimalarial activity (Kwong *et a*l., 2006).

Marine Sponges

Marine sponges are one of the most important diverse sources of several chemical constituents with more therapeutic values. More than 30 % chemical components have been isolated from the sponges. The anticancer drug namely, Ara-C, is strongly used in treating the acute myelocytic leukemia and non-Hodgkin's lymphoma (Turner and Tester, 1997). Moreover, this drug Ara-A, is used for the treating the herpes viral infections. Both Ara-C and Ara-A drugs are prepared from the nucleosides isolated from aa marine sponge. The deep water sponge *Lissodendoryx* sp. can produce the compounds like discodermolide, halichondrin B, that can blocks the cell division by disruption of microtubule structure. Discodermolide is isolated from deep-water sponges *Discodermia* . It has a strong and potent immunosuppressive and anticancer potential. Hence, it inhibits the proliferation of cells by interfering with the cell's microtubule network (HHMI, 1998).

Marine Bryozoan and Ascidian

The chemical component called Bryostatin, is isolated from the bryozoan *Bugulaneritina*. This is a polyketide, possessing specific anticancer and immune enhancing proficiency. Bryostatin works under the activation of protein kinase C with the modulation of cell signaling pathways (Elsberry *et al.*, 1976). This has a specific impact on non-Hodgkin's lymphoma, chronic lymphocyte leukemia, and multiple myeloma disorders. Ecteinascidin 743 is an alkaloid compound, derived from the ascidian *Ecteinascidia turbinate.* It has specific impact on ovarian disorders and other tumours.

Marine Jelly Fish

Aequorin, is a therapeutic compound isolated from a bioluminiscent jellyfish *Aequora victoria.* It is widely and extensively used because of its specific and unique property of emitting light in the presence of calcium. Aequorin has a great impact in illuminating the calcium wave during sea urchin egg fertilization (Chapman *et al.*, 2015). The photoprotein component of aequorin has been cloned into gene expression vectors, and is currently used to monitor calcium in the cytoplasm and organelles of tissue culture cells. Recently, there is new product produced from the bioluminescent jellyfish *A. victoria*, the cloning of green fluorescent protein (GFP). In jellyfish, GFP can absorb the blue light produced by the specific component aequorin and fluoresces green light. GFP is mainly used as a reporter gene in gene regulation studies like expression of genes.

Marine Microalgae

Cyanobacteria are a diverse group of Gram-Negative bacteria, also known as blue-green algae that produce bulk of secondary metabolites with antifungal, antiviral, antibiotic, and other properties. They also exhibit selective bioactivity against vertebrates, invertebrates, plants, microalgae, fungi, bacteria, viruses, and cell lines.

Ulithiacyclamide and Patellamide A produced by *Cyanobacteria* possess potent antimalarial, antitumor, and multidrug resistant activities. Viridamide A produced by *Oscillatoria nigroviridis* showed antitrypanosomal, and antileishmanial activity. *Cladophora rupestris, Codium fragile*s, *Ulva intestinalis,* and *Ulva lactuca* were found to exhibit antiprotozoal activity (Chapman *et al.*, 2015).

Eicosapentaenoic acid (EPA) from the marine diatom, showed activity against Gram-positive and Gram-negative bacteria, methicillin-resistant *Staphylococcus aureus*etc. Microalgae are rich sources of all the vital nutrients such as beta-carotene, vitamins C, A, E, H, B1 , B2, B6, and B12, astaxanthin, polysaccharides, and polyunsaturated fatty acids. Thus, they are widely used as food additives, infant milk formulations, and dietary supplements (Kwong *et al.*, 2006).

Marine Macroalgae

Macroalgae, are seaweeds, that are most popularly used in the nutraceutical industry. They are specifically used in variety of food and food ingredients, especially in Asian countries like Korea, Japan, and China. Macroalgae are the well-known producer of agarose. They are also an important source of many bioactive metabolites with nutritional and therapeutic functions. The bioactive constituents are proteins, furanone, polyunsaturated fatty acids (PUFA), L-α kainic acid, phenotics, pigments, phlorotannins, phyco-colloids (carrageenan and agar), and minerals. The red and brown seaweeds are also good sources of vitamins, minerals, proteins, and essential fatty acids (Zilinskas *et al.*, 1995). They are used to improve protein digestibility. Vitamin E, Vitamin C and alpha-carotene, helps in improving antioxidant defenses in the body. Fat soluble Vitamin K isolated from *Pavlova* helps in blood clotting or coagulation. *Gracilaria edulis* showed the presence of alkaloids, saponin, phenols, terpenoids, proteins, flavonoids, glycosides, coumarins, and tannins. The red algae had significant antibacterial activity against *Pseudomonas aeruginosa, Staphylococcus aureus, Bacillus cereus, Bacillus subtilis, Streptococcus pyogenes, Salmonella typhi* and the fungus *Aspergillus niger, Aspergillus flavus, Rhizopus indicus*, and

Candida albicans. *Sargassum angustifolium, Sargassum oligocystum,* and *Sargassum boveanum* has cytotoxicity and antioxidant potential. *Sargassum angustifolium* showed the highest antioxidant activity. *Tetraselmis* sp., *Dunaliella* sp., *Chlorella* sp., *Synechocystis* sp., and *Oscillatoria* sp. has more antimicrobial activity.

3. Conclusion

The marine environment is vast and harbors different forms of microbial flora and fauna that has the capacity to produce a wide array of bioactive metabolites that is useful for the human mankind, both in nutrition and pharmaceuticals.

4. References

1) Anderson, D. M. (1995). Toxic red tides and harmful algal blooms: A practical challenge in coastal oceanography. *Rev. Geophysics, Suppl. 'U.S. National Report to the Int. Union of Geodesy and Geophysics 1991–1994.* pp.1189–1200.
2) Chapman, A. S., P. Stévant, W. E. Larssen, P. Stévant and W. E. Larssen. (2015). Food or fad? Challenges and opportunities for including seaweeds in a Nordic diet. *Botanica Marina*, 58: 423 - 433.
3) Delaney, J. E. (1985). *Laboratory Procedures for the Examination of Seawater & Shellfish*. A.E. Greenbery, editor; and D.A. Hunt, Washington, DC: Am. Publ. Health Assoc. pp. 64 - 80.
4) Elsberry, R. L., T.S. Friam, and R. N. J. Trapnell. (1976). A mixed layer model of the oceanic thermal response to hurricanes. *Journal of Geophysical Research,* 81: 1153 – 1162.
5) Gai, Y., L. L. Zhao, C. Q. Hu, H. P. Zhang and E. Fusarielin. (2007). A new antifungal antibiotic from *Fusarium* sp. *Chinese Chemical Letters*, 18: 954 - 956.
6) Inagaki, F., T. Nunoura, S. Nakagawa, A. Teske, M. Lever and A. Lauer. (2006). Biogeographical distribution and diversity of microbes in methane hydrate-bearing deep marine sediments on the Pacific Ocean margin. *Proceedings of the National Academy of Sciences of the United States of America*, 103: 2815 - 2820.
7) Kwong, T. F., L. Miao, X. Li and P. Y. Qian. (2006). Novel antifouling and antimicrobial compound from a marine-derived fungus *Ampelomyces* sp. *Marine Biotechnology*, 8: 634 - 640.
8) Li, X., S. K. Kim, K. W. Nam and J. S. Kang, H. D. Choi and B. W. Son. (2006). A new antibacterial dioxopiperazine alkaloid related to gliotoxin from a marine isolate of the fungus *Pseudallescheria*. *Journal of Antibiotics (Tokyo)*, 59: 248 - 250.

9) Trischman, J. A., D. M. Tapiolas, P. R. Jensen, R. Dwight, T. C. McKee and C. M. Ireland. (1994). Salinamides A and B: Anti-inflammatory depsipeptides from a marine *Streptomyces*. *Journal of the American Chemical Society*, 116: 757 - 758.
10) Turner, J. T and P. A. Tester. (1997). Toxic marine phytoplankton, zooplankton grazers, and pelagic food webs. *Limnology and Oceanography*, 42: 1203 – 1214.
11) Winston, J. E. (1988). Biomedical Importance of Marine Organisms. D.G. Fautin, editor, San Francisco: California Academy of Sciences. pp. 1 – 6.
12) Xiong, H., S. Qi, Y. Xu, M. Li and P. Y. Qian. (2009). Antibiotic and antifouling compound production by the marine derived fungus *Cladosporium* sp. F14. *Journal of Hydro-Environment Research*, 2: 264 – 270.
13) Zilinskas, R. A., R. R. Colwell, D. W. Lipton and R. T. Hill. (1995). The Global Challenge of Marine Biotechnology. College Park, Maryland: Maryland Sea Grant College. pp. ix, x, 126.

Advances in Pharmaceutical Sciences
ISBN: 978-81-951323-7-9
First Edition; Volume – 1; 2021
Chapter – 5, Page: 46 - 57

5

ETHANOBOTANICAL USES OF *Swertia chirayita*

Abhishek Amit[1] and Ashish Kumar Singh[2]

[1]Department of Microbiology, School of Life Sciences, Sikkim University (A Central University), Samdur Sikkim, India

[2]Department of Industrial Microbiology, Jagatpur PG College, Jagatpur, Varanasi, India

*Corresponding author: abhishekamit62@gmail.com

Abstract

Swertia chirayita (Gentianaceae), a popular healthful herb native to the temperate, the Himalaya is utilized in ancient drugs to treat various ailments like liver disorders, malaria, and polygenic disease and area unit rumoured to possess a decent spectrum of medicine properties. Its healthful usage is well-documented in Indian pharmaceutical codex, British, and so the yank pharmacopoeias and in many ancient drugs just like the Ayurveda, Unani, Siddha, and alternative standard medical systems. This ethnomedicinal herb is understood principally for its bitter style caused by the presence of various bioactive compounds that area unit directly related to human health welfare. The increasing high usage of *Swertia chirayita*, principally the underground tissues, additionally as a result of the bootleg overharvesting combined with home ground destruction resulted throughout a forceful reduction of its populations and has brought this plant to the verge of extinction. The increasing national and international demand for *Swertia chirayita* has semiconductor diode to unscrupulous assortment from the wild and adulteration of providers. The aim of this review is to produce a synthesis of this state of information domain on the healthful uses, phytochemistry, medicine activities of *Swertia chirayita* and to spotlight its future prospects. Medicine knowledge rumoured in literature recommend that *Swertia chirayita* shows a helpful impact among the treatment of many ailments. However, there is lack of adequate data on the protection analysis of the plant. The medicine utility of *Swertia chirayita* needs the requirement for conservation friendly approaches in its utilization. However, a lot of advanced analysis is secure to work out the activities of bioactive compounds *in vitro* and *in vivo*, establish their underlying mechanisms of action and begin the method of clinical analysis.

Key words: Ethnobotany, Medicinal plants, Medicinal uses and *Swertia chirayita*.

1. Introduction

One of the stipulations for the success of primary health care is that the convenience and use of appropriate medication. ancient drugs continue to be the foremost reasonable and simply accessible supply of treatment within the primary care system. medicative plants have forever been a possible supply to cure totally different diseases, either within the style of ancient preparations or as pure active principles, and that they square measure often the sole supply of medication for the bulk of individuals within the developing world. However, a comprehensive review detailing the documented ethnomedicinal uses, pharmacological properties and safety evaluation carried out on *Swertia chirayita* and identifying the existing knowledge gap is lacking. In this review, we document the medicinal uses and phytochemical properties of *Swertia chirayita*.

2. Vernacular Names

English: Chirata (Indian Gentian)
Hindi: Charayatah
Urdu: Chiarayata,
Sanskrit: Anaryatikta, Bhunimba, Chiratika, Ardhatika, Varantaka,
Arabic: Qasabuzzarirah
Persian: Nenilawandi, Qasabuzzarirah
Panjabi: Charaita
Bengali: Chireta
Burma: Sekhagi
Marathi: Chirayita
Tamil: Nilavembu, Shirattakuchi
Telugu: Nilavembu
Kannada: Nilavebu
Malayalam: Nilaveppa
Gujarati: Chirayata
Nepal: Cherata
Deccan: Charayatah

3. Taxonomical Classification

Kingdom: Plantae
Phylum: Tracheophyta
Class: Magnoliopsida
Order: Gentianales
Family: Gentianaceae
Genus: Swertia
Spicies: Chirata
Binomial name: *Swertia chirata*

Figure - 1: Swertia chirayita (a) Seed (b) Plant in nature (c) Root of a mature plant (d) Dry plant material (d) High shoot multiplication in plant tissue culture.

4. Period of Occurrence

The plant quickly spreads from seed which is shed during October and November. Herbs can be cultivated in suitable localities in the temperate Himalayas. Seeds are very small in size, should be sown in nursery and seedlings transplanted later in the field.

5. Distribution

It is endemic to the mountainous districts of northern Asian country, Temperate Himalaya Mountains at altitudes between one, 200 - 3,000 m from Kashmir to Kingdom of Bhutan and in Khasi hills in Meghalaya at 1200 – 1500 m. It happens as entire plants or as a broken piece of plant. The stem is swish with skinny pronto dissociable bark, up to 1m long, outwardly it's chromatic or violet brown in colour. It is cylindrical in basal region, polygonal shape with ascending branches, wood of stem is porous and yellow, enclosure within the intermodal regions. giant chromatic simply dissociable pith is found during this plant with easy root, round shape with few slender rootlets. The leaves area unit opposite sessile, entire ovate lanceolate; 5 - nerved with rounded base, acuminate apex and full margin panicles; coil and gyre every 4 - compound, stamens 4, perigynous; ovary unilocular with 2 membrane bone placentae; vogue slender with recurred stigmas, fruit associate degree ovoid brownness unilocular several seeded capsule, odour is bedimmed and style is incredibly bitter (Kirtiker *et al.*, 1996)

Figure - 2: Natural distribution of Swertia chirayita. The shaded area represents the natural habitat

6. Ethnobotanical Description

All components of the chirayita plant square measure helpful for therapeutic functions. It's a specific kind of bright chromatic colour everywhere the herb in contemporary sample. The surface of stem is sleek and while not hairs or projections, and might be up to one m long and half-dozen millimetre in diameter and yellowish-brown to chromatic in colour. The higher a part of stem is slightly quadrilateral and its lower part is cylindrical; giant, continuous and without delay detachable yellow pith. The leaves of the plant square measure cauline, opposite, broad at base, smoothened surface, of a slim oval form tapering to a degree at every finish, acuminate, usually with 5-7 simply recognizable lateral veins. The flowers square measure multilateral and therefore the shapes square measure oval, 2-3 millimetre wide, with 2 organ depressions close to the bottom of every of curl lobes. The ovary is oval formed and pointed, having 2 carpels, characterised by only 1 loculus; fruit a capsule with many small netlike seed around 0.25 millimetre long and zero.16 mm to 0.45 millimetre in width with irregular oval shape (Department of AYUSH Ministry of Health & Family Welfare, Government of India, 2007 and 1992)

7. Phytochemistry

The widespread uses of *S. chirayita* as a standard drug and its exploitation in trendy medical systems have crystal rectifier to an increase in scientific exploration of its phytochemistry so as to spot the active phytochemicals. This has resulted during an extended body of literature exploring the chemical constituents of this plant (Mandal *et al.,* 1987; Chakravarty *et al.,* 1991, 1994; Mandal *et al.,* 1992; Chatterjee and Pakrashi, 1995; Pant *et al.,* 2000). The wide-range biological activities of S. chirayita square measure attributed to the presence of a various cluster of pharmacologically bioactive compounds happiness to completely different categories like xanthones and their derivatives, lignans, alkaloids, flavonoids, terpenoids, iridoids, secoiridoids, and different compounds like chiratin, ophelic acid, saturated fatty acid, oleic acid, and saturated fatty acid (Pant *et al.,* 2000; Patil *et al.,* 2013). the primary isolated dimeric xanthone was chiratanin gift in several elements of *S. chirayita*. The medical specialty efficaciousness of S. chirayita has been part attributed to the biological activity of major phytoconstituents together with amarogentin, swertiamarin, mangiferin, swerchirin, sweroside, amaroswerin, and gentiopicrin. Amarogentin is according to be medication (Phoboo *et al.,* 2013), anticancerous (Saha *et al.,* 2006; Pal *et al.,* 2012), and antileishmanial (Ray *et al.,* 1996; Medda *et al.,* 1999), whereas swertiamarin has been tested for its anti-hepatitis (Wang *et al.,* 2001), anti-tumour (Kavimani *et al.,* 2000), anti-arthritic activities (Saravanan *et al.,* 2014). it's been shown to exhibit anti-diabetic (Vaidya *et al.,* 2013) properties. Mangiferin is additionally according to own anti-diabetic, anti-atherosclerotic (Pardo-Andreu *et al.,* 2008), anticancer, anti-HIV (Guha *et al.,* 1996), anti-Parkinson (Kavitha *et al.,* 2013), and chemo preventive (Yoshimi *et al.,* 2001) activities. Swerchirin is thought to be antiprotozoal, hypoglycaemic (Bajpai *et al.,* 1991; Saxena *et al.,* 1996), hepato-protective, pro-haematopoietic (Ya *et al.,* 1999), with glucose lowering activity (Sekar *et al.,* 1987; Saxena *et al.,* 1991) and weak chemo preventive medical specialty effects (Hirakawa *et al.,* 2005). Swerchirin at completely different concentrations (1, 10, and a hundred μm) considerably increased aldohexose stirred internal secretion unleash from isolated islets (Saxena *et al.,* 1993). Sweroside is according to be medicine (Siler *et al.,* 2010), hepatoprotective (Liu *et al.,* 1994; Luo *et al.,* 2009), preventative in treatment for physiological state (Jeong *et al.,* 2015), and is additionally urged as a promising pathology therapeutic natural product (Sun *et al.,* 2013). Amaroswerin is thought for its gastroprotective effects of the bitter principles (Niiho *et al.,* 2006).

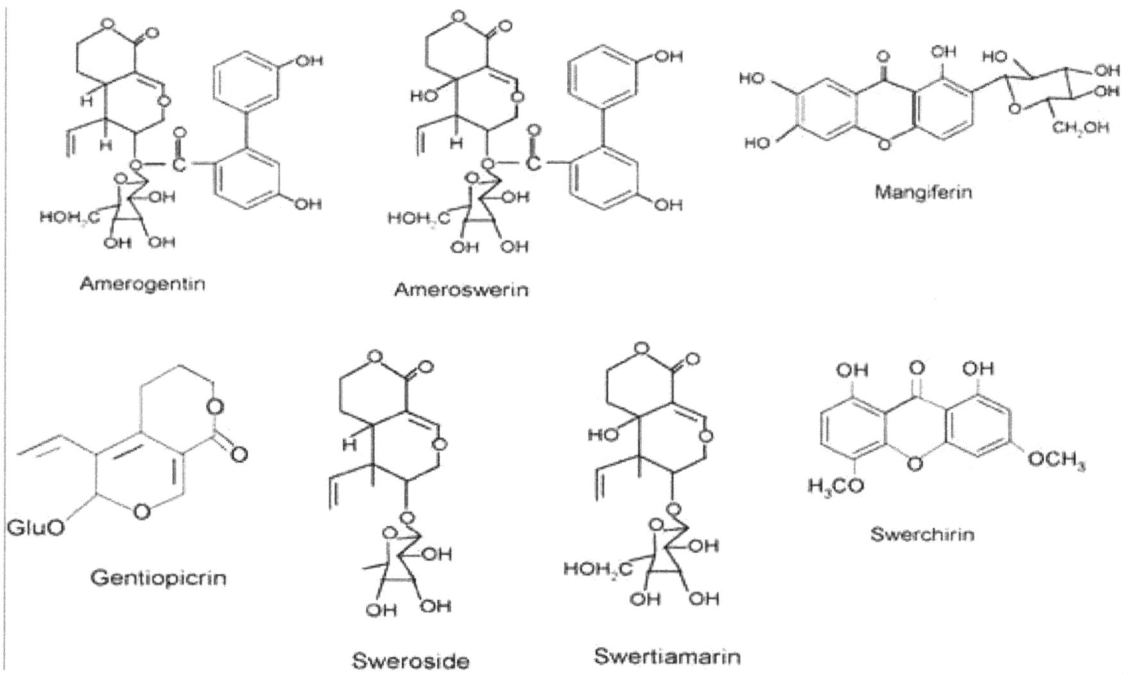

Figure - 3: Chemical structures of important phytoconstituents found in Swertia chirayita

8. Pharmacological Studies

- Antibacterial Activity
- Antifungal Activity
- Antiviral Activity
- Antioxidant Activity
- Anti-inflammatory Activity
- Hypoglycaemic Activity
- Anti-diabetic Activity
- Anti-malarial Activity
- Hepatoprotective Activity
- Anti-leishmanial Activity
- Anti-carcinogenic Activity
- Anthelmintic Activity
- Anti-pyretic Activity
- Antidiarrheal Activity
- Anti-HIV
- CNS depressant Activity
- Mutagenicity Activity
- Anti-leprosy Activity

- Anti-cholinergic Activity
- Anti-hepatitis B Virus Activity
- Dyslipidaemia
- Gastroprotective Activity
- Wound Healing Activity

9. Medicinal Use

Table - 1: Ethnobotanical uses of Swertia chirayita in traditional medicine

Plant part used	Traditional uses	References
Whole plant	Used in several traditional and indigenous systems of medicines, such as Ayurveda, Unani, and Siddha	Mukherji (1953); Kirtikar and Basu (1984); Joshi and Dhawan (2005)
Whole plant	Used in British and American pharmacopoeias as tinctures and infusions	Joshi and Dhawan (2005)
Root	Serves as a drug and an effective tonic for general weakness, fever, cough, joint pain, asthma, and the common cold	Kirtikar and Basu (1984); Joshi and Dhawan (2005)
Whole plant	For headaches and blood pressure, the leaves and chopped stems are soaked overnight in water. A paste is prepared and filtered with 1 glass of water. The preparation is consumed once a day for 2 – 3 days	de Rus Jacquet *et al.* (2014); Malla *et al.* (2015)
Whole plant	For Tremor fever, whole *Swertia chirayita* plants are cut into small pieces and boiled in 1/2 L of water until the volume is reduced to less than half glass. The filtered water is stored in a glass bottle and half spoon is given to children once a day for 2 days. For adult, the posology is 1 spoon once in a day for 2 days and varies to three times a day until cured	de Rus Jacquet *et al.* (2014)
Whole plant	Boiled in water and one cup of decoction is taken orally to cure malaria	Shah *et al.* (2014)
Whole plant	Paste of the plant is applied to treat skin diseases such as eczema and pimples	Joshi and Dhawan (2005); Malla *et al.* (2015)
Whole plant	Liver disorders; stomach disorders like dyspepsia and diarrhoea, intestinal worms	Mukherji (1953); Joshi and Dhawan (2005)
Whole plant	Hiccups and vomiting, ulcers, gastrointestinal infections, and kidney diseases	Kirtikar and Basu (1984)
Whole plant	Used in combination with other drugs in cases of scorpion bite	Nandkarni (1976)
Whole plant	Used in excessive vaginal discharge	Jadhav and Bhutani (2005)

10. Conclusions and Future Perspectives

Swertia chirayita offers several promising prospects for each ancient and fashionable drugs. *Swertia chirayita* is seemingly a possible therapy for several ailments. This review summarized the prevailing ethnobotanical uses, phytochemistry, medical specialty activities, safety analysis, and conservation standing on *Swertia chirayita*. So far, no serious aspect effects or toxicity of dicot genus chirayita are reported, however any toxicologic studies are still required to substantiate the protection of dicot genus chirayita in humans. Efforts are needed for any studies, particularly evaluating its biological activities in vivo and toxicologic and agent properties so as to raised validate the protection of those completely different plant-derives compounds. altogether likelihood there's a necessity for clinical trials to determine the efficaciousness of victimization dicot genus chirayita in drugs. because of its multiple uses the demand in each national and international markets is continually on the increase. Over utilization combined with surround destruction has resulted within the forceful reduction of its population. For the in exploitation of this critically vulnerable medicative plant any projected analysis should be viewed during a wider context that has conservation practices and property offer of raw plants. this can need innovative tools, that utilize biotechnological interventions, as well as micropropagation, cryopreservation, and bioreactors for the conservation, similarly as for raising industrial production. In artificial seed technology additional elaborated analysis is needed principally for improvement in germination frequency of artificial seeds and sequent plant growth in soil so it is often used on an advertisement scale. to boot, within the close to future, crown gall technology is often used as a model system and can conjointly offer plant biotechnologists with powerful tools to boost the precious phytochemicals of dicot genus chirayita. though economical micropropagation protocols are established, any studies that specialize in seed biology and ways in which of up bioactive secondary metabolites in cultivated dicot genus *Chirayita* would be helpful for his or her exploitation. internal control protocols to stop misidentification and attainable adulteration of dicot genus chirayita also are required. In summary, dicot genus chirayita are studied extensively in terms of taxonomy, ethnobotany, phytochemistry, biological activities, and conservation. However, new findings might increase the current therapeutic importance of dicot genus chirayita and promote their future use in fashionable drugs, whereas novel biotechnological approaches are needed for any conservation.

11. References

1) Anonymous. 1992. The Unani Pharmacopoeia of India, CCRUM, (Vol. 2) Department of AYUSH Ministry of Health & Family Welfare, Government of India Seema Offset Press New Delhi-110006. pp.117-125
2) Anonymous. 2007. The Unani Pharmacopoeia of India, CCRUM, 2007; Department of AYUSH Ministry of Health & Family Welfare, Government of India Rakmo Press New Delhi - 110 020.
3) Bajpai MB, Asthana RK, Sharma NK, Chatterjee SK and Mukherjee SK. 1991. Hypoglycemic effect of Swerchirin from the hexane fraction of *Swertia chirayita*. *Planta Medica*, 57(02): 102 - 104.
4) Chakravarty AK, Mukhopadhyay S and Das B. 1991. Swertane triterpenoids from *Swertia chirata*. *Phytochemistry*, 30(12): 4087 - 4092.
5) Chakravarty AK, Mukhopadhyay S, Moitra SK and Das B. 1994. Syringaresinol, a hepatoprotective agent and other constituents from *Swertia chirata*. *Indian Journal of Chemistry. Sect. B: Organic Chemistry, including Medical Chemistry*, 33(4): 405 - 408.
6) Chatterjee A and Pakrashi SC. 1995. Treatise on Indian medicinal plants, vol III. *Publications and Information Directorate, CSIR, New Delhi,* 5: 60 - 71.
7) de Rus Jacquet A, Subedi R, Ghimire SK and Rochet JC. 2014. Nepalese traditional medicine and symptoms related to Parkinson' s disease and other disorders: Patterns of the usage of plant resources along the Himalayan altitudinal range. *Journal of Ethnopharmacology,* 153(1): 178 - 189.
8) Guha S, Ghosal S and Chattopadhyay U. 1996. Antitumor, immunomodulatory and anti-HIV effect of Mangiferin, a naturally occurring glucosylxanthone. *Chemotherapy*, 42(6): 443 - 451.
9) Hirakawa K, Yoshida M, Nagatsu A, Mizukami H, Rana V, Rawat MS, Oikawa S and Kawanishi S. 2005. Chemopreventive action of xanthone derivatives on photosensitized DNA damage. *Photochemistry and Photobiology*, 81(2): 314 - 319.
10) Jadhav AN and Bhutani KK. 2020. Ayurveda and gynecological disorders. *Journal of Ethnopharmacology,* 97(1): 151 - 159.
11) Jeong YT, Jeong SC, Hwang JS and Kim JH. 2015. Modulation effects of sweroside isolated from the Lonicera japonica on melanin synthesis. *Chemico-biological Interactions,* 238: 33 - 39.
12) Jie L, Yaping L and Klaassen CD. 1994. The effect of Chinese hepatoprotective medicines on experimental liver injury in mice. *Journal of Ethnopharmacology*, 42(3): 183 - 191.
13) Joshi P and Dhawan V. 2005. *Swertia chirayita* – an overview. *Current Science*, 635 - 640.

14) Kavimani S, Manisenthlkumar KT. 2000. Effect of methanolic extract of *Enicostemma littorale* on Dalton's ascitic lymphoma. *Journal of Ethnopharmacology*, 71(1-2): 349 - 352.
15) Kavitha M, Nataraj J, Essa MM, Memon MA and Manivasagam T. 2013. Mangiferin attenuates MPTP induced dopaminergic neurodegeneration and improves motor impairment, redox balance and Bcl-2/Bax expression in experimental Parkinson's disease mice. *Chemico-biological Interactions*, 206(2): 239 - 247.
16) Kirtiker K. B. 1996. Indian Medicinal Plants (2 ed., Vol. 3). Dehradun: International Book Distributors, Rajpur road, Dehradun, India. pp. 1664 - 1666.
17) Kumar V and Van Staden J. 2016. A review of *Swertia chirayita* (Gentianaceae) as a traditional medicinal plant. *Frontiers in Pharmacology*, 6: 308 - 315.
18) Luo YD, Chen J, Cao J, Wen XD and Li P. 2009. Determination of sweroside in rat plasma and bile for oral bioavailability and hepatobiliary excretion. *Chemical and Pharmaceutical Bulletin*, 57(1): 79 - 83.
19) Malla B, Gauchan DP and Chhetri RB. 2015. An ethnobotanical study of medicinal plants used by ethnic people in Parbat district of western Nepal. *Journal of Ethnopharmacology*, 165: 103 - 117.
20) Mandal S and Chatterjee A. 1987. Structure of chiratanin, a novel dimeric xanthone. *Tetrahedron Letters*, 28(12): 1309 - 1310.
21) Mandal S, Das PC, Joshi PC, Chatterjee A, Islam CS, Dutta MR, Patra BD and Sikdar S. 1992. Anti-inflammatory action of *Swertia chirata*. *Fitoterapia LXIII*, 122–128.
22) Medda S, Mukhopadhyay S and Basu MK. 1999. Evaluation of the *in vivo* activity and toxicity of amarogentin, an antileishmanial agent, in both liposomal and niosomal forms. *Journal of Antimicrobial Chemotherapy*, 44(6): 791 - 794.
23) Mukherji B. 1953. *Indian Pharmaceutical Codex*. CSIR.
24) Niiho Y, Yamazaki T, Nakajima Y, Yamamoto T, Ando H, Hirai Y, Toriizuka K and Ida Y. 2006. Gastroprotective effects of bitter principles isolated from Gentian root and Swertia herb on experimentally-induced gastric lesions in rats. *Journal of Natural Medicines,* 60(1): 82 - 88.
25) Pal D, Sur S, Mandal S, Das A, Roy A, Das S and Panda CK. (2012). Prevention of liver carcinogenesis by amarogentin through modulation of G 1/S cell cycle check point and induction of apoptosis. *Carcinogenesis*, 33(12): 2424 - 2431.

26) Pardo-Andreu GL, Paim BA, Castilho RF, Velho JA, Delgado R, Vercesi AE and Oliveira HC. 2008. *Mangifera indica* L. extract (Vimang®) and its main polyphenol mangiferin prevent mitochondrial oxidative stress in atherosclerosis-prone hypercholesterolemic mouse. *Pharmacological Research*, 57(5): 332 - 338.
27) Patil K, Dhande S and Kadam V. 2013. Therapeutic *Swertia chirata* - an overview. *Research Journal of Pharmacogenetics and Phytochemistry,* 5: 199 - 207.
28) Phoboo S, Pinto MD, Barbosa AC, Sarkar D, Bhowmik PC, Jha PK and Shetty K. 2013. Phenolic-Linked Biochemical Rationale for the Anti-Diabetic Properties of Swertia chirayita (*Roxb. ex Flem.*) *Karst*. *Phytotherapy Research*, 27(2): 227 - 235.
29) Ray S, Majumder HK, Chakravarty AK, Mukhopadhyay S, Gil RR and Cordell GA. 1996. Amarogentin, a naturally occurring secoiridoid glycoside and a newly recognized inhibitor of topoisomerase I from *Leishmania donovani*. *Journal of Natural Products*, 59(1): 27 - 39.
30) Saha P, Mandal S, Das A and Das S. 2006. Amarogentin can reduce hyperproliferation by downregulation of Cox-II and upregulation of apoptosis in mouse skin carcinogenesis model. *Cancer Letters*, 244(2): 252 - 259.
31) Saravanan S, Islam VH, Babu NP, Pandikumar P, Thirugnanasambantham K, Chellappandian M, Raj CS, Paulraj MG and Ignacimuthu S. 2014. *Swertiamarin attenuates* inflammation mediators via modulating NF-κB/I κB and JAK2/STAT3 transcription factors in adjuvant induced arthritis. *European Journal of Pharmaceutical Sciences*, 56: 70 - 86.
32) Saxena AM, Bajpai MB and Mukherjee SK. 1991. Swerchirin induced blood sugar lowering of streptozotocin treated hyperglycemic rats. *Indian Journal of Experimental Biology,* 29(7): 674 - 675.
33) Saxena AM, Bajpai MB, Murthy PS and Mukherjee SK. 1993. Mechanism of blood sugar lowering by a Swerchirin-containing hexane fraction (SWI) of *Swertia chirayita*. *Indian Journal of Experimental Biology*, 31(2): 178 - 181.
34) Saxena AM, Murthy PS and Mukherjee SK. 1996. Mode of action of three structurally different hypoglycemic agents: a comparative study. *Indian Journal of Experimental Biology*, 34(4): 351 - 365.
35) Sekar BC, Mukherjee B, Chakravarti RB and Mukherjee SK. 1987. Effect of different fractions of Swertia chirayita on the blood sugar level of albino rats. *Journal of Ethnopharmacology*, 21(2): 175 - 181.
36) Shah GM, Abbasi AM, Khan N, Guo X, Khan MA, Hussain M, Bibi S, Nazir A and Tahir AA. 2014. Traditional uses of medicinal plants against malarial disease by the tribal communities of Lesser Himalayas–Pakistan. *Journal of Ethnopharmacology*, 155(1): 450 - 462.

37) Šiler B, Mišić D, Nestorović J, Banjanac T, Glamočlija J, Soković M and Ćirić A. 2010. Antibacterial and antifungal screening of *Centaurium pulchellum* crude extracts and main secoiridoid compounds. *Natural Product Communications*, 5(10): 1934 – 1940.
38) Sun H, Li L, Zhang A, Zhang N, Lv H, Sun W and Wang X. 2013. Protective effects of sweroside on human MG-63 cells and rat osteoblasts. *Fitoterapia*, 84: 174 - 179.
39) Vaidya H, Goyal RK and Cheema SK. (2013). Anti-diabetic Activity of Swertiamarin is due to an Active Metabolite, Gentianine, that Upregulates PPAR-γ Gene Expression in 3T3-L1 cells. *Phytotherapy Research*, 27(4): 624 - 627.
40) Wang CZ, Maier UH, Eisenreich W, Adam P, Obersteiner I, Keil M, Bacher A and Zenk MH. 2001. Unexpected biosynthetic precursors of amarogentin - a retrobiosynthetic 13C NMR study. *European Journal of Organic Chemistry*, 2001(8): 1459 - 1465.
41) Ya BQ, Nian LC, Li C and Gen XP. 1999. Protective effect of swerchirin on hematopoiesis in 60Co-irradiated mice. *Phytomedicine,* 6(2): 85 - 88.
42) Yoshimi N, Matsunaga K, Katayama M, Yamada Y, Kuno T, Qiao Z, Hara A, Yamahara J and Mori H. 2001. The inhibitory effects of mangiferin, a naturally occurring glucosylxanthone, in bowel carcinogenesis of male F344 rats. *Cancer Letters*, 163(2): 163 - 170.

Advances in Pharmaceutical Sciences
ISBN: 978-81-951323-7-9
First Edition; Volume – 1; 2021
Chapter – 6, Page: 58 - 66

6

PHARMACOLOGICAL BENEFITS OF Eleutherococcus senticosus

B. Sindhuja*, J. Rengaramanujam and J. Devakumar

Department of Microbiology, Dr.N.G.P. Arts and Science College (An Autonomous Institution), Coimbatore – 641 048, Tamil Nadu, India.

*Corresponding author: sindhubaskaran95@gmail.com

Abstract

Eleutherococcus senticosus Harms, called Siberian ginseng is a medicinal plant with a long history of use (by the Chinese for over 2000 years). Eleuthero can reach a height of six feet, although it grows slowly. It usually flowers in July, depending on the climate. The flowers are self-fertile and may also be pollinated by insects. Root extracts of *Echinococcus senticosus* are sold as a dietary supplement or cosmetic, usually under the name *Siberian ginseng.* Eleuthero contains eleutherosides-eleutherosides B (syringin) and E (syringaresinol) that are used to identify *Siberian ginseng*. It is also used to boost immunity, and as an antimicrobial and chemoprotectant. The correct dose for you may depend on factors including your age, gender, and medical history. In order to achieve this status a plant must be harmless to the body. It must also have a broad-spectrum, normalizing action that brings an organism back to homeostasis. Through Russian Research, Eleuthero became the model for all other adaptogens. In the late '60's and '70's, studies were conducted in over 2,100 healthy people. Another study found that healthy people who took *Siberian ginseng* for 4 weeks had more T-cells, which may indicate their immune systems were stronger. One double-blind study of 93 people with Herpes Simplex Virus (HSV) Type 2, which can cause genital herpes, found that taking *Siberian ginseng* reduced the number of outbreaks. These studies showed that Eleuthero increased the ability of subjects to withstand stress such as heat, noise, motion, exercise, and increase in workload. Subjects also experienced a normalization in mental alertness and work output.

Key words: *Eleutherococcus senticosus, Siberian ginseng*, Root, Immunity and Mental alertness.

1. Introduction

Plant-based products have been used to manage various ailments for the centuries in different ethnic communities of the world. Nowadays, such products are used in developed and developing countries separately and/or together with synthetic drugs. It is established that about 120 plant derived compounds are used in western medicine, and about 80 % of the world population uses medicinal plants in primary health care (Verpoorte *et al.,* 2000).

Eleutherococcus senticosus is a species of small, woody shrub in the family Araliaceae native to North-eastern Asia (Figure - 1). It may be colloquially called devil's bush, Siberian ginseng, eleuthero, *ciwujia*, *Devil's shrub*, *shigoka*, *touch-me-not*, *wild pepper*, or *kanjang*. Eleuthero has been traditionally used as an immune system booster and a general stimulant and used for the treatment of inflammatory diseases, anemia, and rheumatoid arthritis. People use the root of the plant to make medicine. Eleuthero is used for diabetes, athletic performance, memory and thinking skills (cognitive function), the common cold, and genital herpes. Many other conditions, but there is no good scientific evidence supporting most of its uses (Yang *et al.,* 2013; Panossian *et al.,* 1999).

In the Chinese and Russian ethnomedicine, its use was empirical, because people used to believe that it was a panacea that promoted longevity, with beneficial effects for the treatment of physical fatigues. The fruits have been used for a long time as an ingredient of the fermented wine, the leaves as a tonic, as a functional beverage marketed for reducing liver damage, and accelerating alcohol detoxification (Jin *et al.,* 2013; Watson *et al.,* 2003).

At present, in China the ethanol extract of the roots is a popular health supplement for weakness, diseases connected with inflammation (rheumatism, haemorrhoids), and impotence. It was reported that, in the Olympic Games, the players of the Old Soviet Union have increased records after administering the *E. senticosus* roots products (Arouca *et al.,* 2013 and Schmidt *et al.,* 2014). According to Załuski's previous studies, the fruits of that species cultivated in Poland, act as antioxidants, inductors of the apoptosis in Jurkat 45 and HL60 leukemic cell lines, and inhibitors of MMP-1, MMP-2, MMP-3, and MMP-9 (Zaluski *et al.,* 2012; Zaluski *et al.,* 2016).

Figure - 1: Eleuthero (Eleutherococcus senticosus)

2. Medicinal properties of Eleutherococcus senticosus

Siberian ginseng supplements are made from the root. The root has a mixture of components called eleutherosides that are thought to have health benefits. Among the other ingredients are chemicals called polysaccharides, which have been found to boost the immune system and lower blood sugar levels in animal tests. The pharmaceutically active components of eleuthero primarily consist of eleutherosides A through M, especially B and E. Additional components include acanthoside D, friedelin and isofraxidin. This large number of active components makes eleuthero useful for supporting a variety of biological functions.

The *Eleutherococcus senticosus* products attract global attention as a novel medicinal plant and since a few years have become popular as dietary supplement in the United States and European countries. Imported products of this plant have become available in North America, with a market share of 3.1 % of the $12 billion medicinal herbal industry. The 1994 DSHEA (Dietary Supplement Health and Education Act) regulation allows a direct commercialization of *E. senticosus* as a supplement for consumption in the United States without the regulation of the FDA (Food and Drug Administration). With the increased awareness of developing countries that the study of traditional medicines and finding new leads is important, there is a need to avoid imported expensive eastern medicines and to estimate a new source of some eastern herbs in Europe. Preparations of the roots of *E. senticosus* are given in cases of asthenia with weakness and fatigue, for example, in convalescence. This indication has been officially accepted by the Community Herbal Monograph on *Eleutherococcus senticosus* (Rupr et Maxim) Maxim Radix (EMEA/HMPC/ 244569/2006), published by the European Medicines Agency. The clinical application of *E. senticosus* is generally considered safe; however, the European

Community Herbal Monograph states "arterial hypertension" as a contraindication (Arouca *et al.,* 2013; Schmidt *et al.,* 2014).

The roots of *E. senticosus* are source of phenols, called eleutherosides (derivatives of lignans, coumarins, and phenylpropanoids), flavonoids (hyperin, rutin, afzelin, quercetin, and kaempferol), phenolic acids, triterpenic acids, and anthocyanins. Compounds isolated from the fruits belong to eleutherosides (eleutherosides B and E), flavonoids, phenolic acids, and essential oil (0.3%, v/d.w.). The dried fruits, consumed as food, are rich in Ca, Mg, Mn, Zn, and Cu. In the leaves, flavonoids (quercetin, quercitrin, and rutin) have been identified (Cheen *et al.,* 2002; Lee *et al.,* 2014; Miho Hatanaka *et al.,* 2017).

3. Pharmacological benefits of Eleutherococcus senticosus

Increasing energy and Reducing fatigue

As a stimulant, eleuthero boosts energy levels and contains compounds known to help overcome exhaustion and prevent its side effects. One study Trusted Source found that eleuthero consumption significantly increased the exhaustion point of swimming mice by lessening the build-up of lactic acid and blood urea nitrogen, in addition to increasing fat utilization.

Improving cognitive function

By increasing circualation, eleuthero may increase blood flow to the brain, improving mental function such as memory and concentration.

Managing cancer

Eleuthero has been shown to have anti-cancer or anti-tumor properties. Research suggests eleuthero may have similar properties, especially in cases of lung cancer, but this claim requires more research.

Treating Parkinson's Disease

According to several animal studies on the supplementation of Eleuthero, the results have shown a reduction in the degenerative effects of Parkinson's disease. However, there is still more research to be conducted to confirm the same effect in human clinical usage.

Enhancing exercise

As a stimulant, eleuthero may increase the ability of muscles to do work, especially during periods of intense physical activity. One study trusted Source found that consuming 800 milligrams (mg) of eleuthero a day for 8 weeks increased a male subject's endurance time by 23 percent, peak oxygen saturation by 12 percent, and highest heart rate by 3 percent (Figure - 2).

Healing wounds and preventing ulcers

By boosting the immune system, eleuthero may improve or speed up the healing process. Compounds in eleuthero have also been shown to prevent the formation of ulcers, including diabetic foot ulcers.

Increasing low blood pressure

As a stimulant, eleuthero increases circulation and heart rate, and may raise blood pressure over time. This may be beneficial for people with low blood pressure, but can cause risks for people with hypertension.

Reducing osteoporosis

In several traditional medicines, eleuthero is used to increase muscle and bone strength. In a 2013 study, rats given 100 mg of eleuthero daily for 8 weeks saw a 16.7 percent increase in femur bone density.

Managing menopause

Extracts of eleuthero and eleutherosides are known to bind to estrogen receptor sites. Eleuthero may, therefore, lessen the effects of estrogen withdrawal in women who are experiencing menopause. For this reason, women with estrogen-driven cancer may need to consult their doctor before consuming eleuthero.

Reducing or limiting respiratory tract infections

As an immune stimulant, eleuthero may shorten the length and severity of lung infections, such as influenza and pneumonia.

Improving lymphatic function

Eleutherosides have been shown to improve the lymphatic function of the lymph node network, meaning they may reduce edema. Edema is swelling caused by a build up of fluid.A 2016 study found eleuthero powder significantly reduced edema within 2 and 4 hours after consumption in 50 healthy volunteers.

Preventing and repairing nerve damage

Several studies have shown that eleutherosides may help prevent and repair nerve damage. Eleuthero has been explored, as a potential preventative or management medication for progressive neurological conditions, such as Alzheimer's disease. One study found that eleuthero improved nerve regeneration and synapse reformation in rats with nerve damage.

Reduces Inflammation

Some pain-relieving drugs like naproxen sodium work by inhibiting the inflammatory pathway activating enzyme, COX-2. Eleuthero has also been found to be associated with reduced expression of COX-2, thus making it a promising agent for preventing inflammation. It also reduces the excess mast cell activity associated with allergic inflammation.

Eleuthero is Antiviral

Following a review of studies where a standardized extract of Eleuthero was used, it was confirmed that this herb is effective in treating herpes simplex 2 and relieves the symptoms of common cold. The liquid extract of Eleuthero has been found to be effective against several RNA viruses, including influenza A virus, respiratory syncytial virus, and human rhinovirus. The herb helps fight against these viruses as it prevents their replication (Glatthaar Saalmüller *et al.*, 2001).

Lowering or Stabilizing blood sugar levels

Eleutherosides have been shown to reduce insulin resistance and are being considered for the management of type 2 diabetes. A 2013 study found that 480 mg per day of eleuthero significantly lowered fasting and post-meal blood sugar levels in subjects with type 2 diabetes. Eleuthero extracts are made using the plant's bark, stems, leaves, or roots. The herb is sold in the form of capsules, tablets, a liquid or tincture, and as a powder. It can also be used whole, and the herb's dried leaves and stems can be boiled to make a tea. The plant's fresh fruit may also be eaten raw. Although, it can be sold alone, eleuthero is also commonly found in multivitamins and tonics aimed at boosting immune function, increasing energy levels, and promoting vitality.

The FDA outlines specific guidelines and regulations for the production, marketing, and sale of herbal supplements. Every product must meet the guideline and regulation in order to be able to sell and market supplement products. The United States Pharmacopeia (USP) is a third party research organization that also tests the quality and safety of dietary and herbal supplements. Eleutherosides, in particular, eleutheroside B, is usually the main bioactive ingredient, and a pharmacist should be able to recommend appropriate products that contain this (Miho Hatanaka *et al.,* 2017).

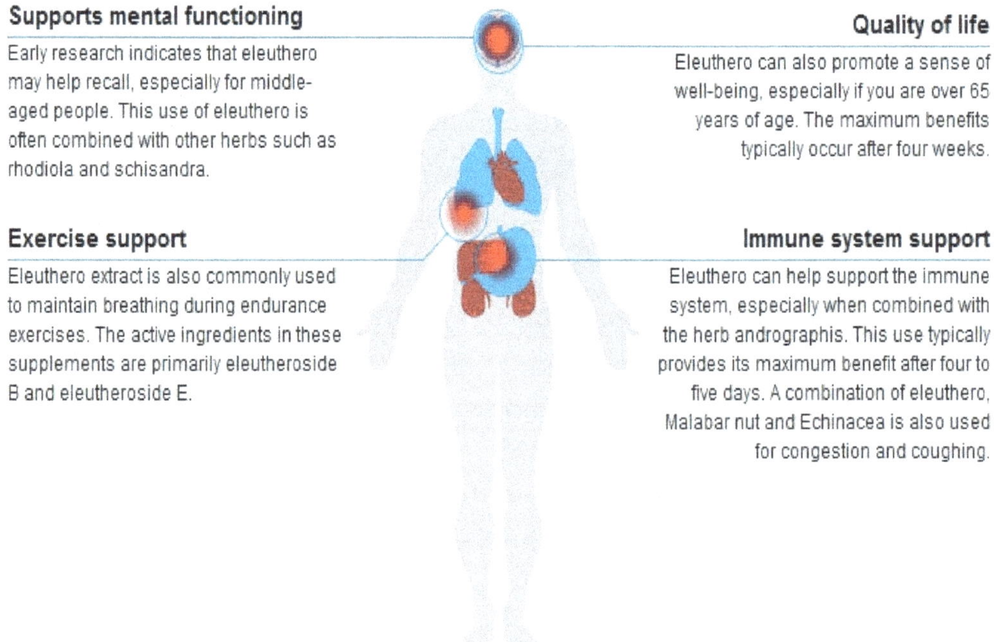

Figure - 2: Pharmacological benefits of Eleutherococcus senticosus

The following oral doses have been studied in scientific research (Jung *et al.,* 2007)

- For diabetes: 480 mg of eleuthero extract, standardized to contain eleutheroside E and B 1.12 %, daily for 3 months.
- For genital herpes: 400 mg of eleuthero extract standardized to contain eleutheroside E 0.3 %, daily for 3 months.
- For cold: take between 300- and 1,200-mg daily, not exceeding 3- to 6-grams
- take in the morning to avoid disrupting the sleep cycle
- take doses between meals
- take the supplement for no more than 6 weeks continuously followed by at least a 2 - 3 week break.

4. Conclusion

The herb *Eleutherococcus senticosus* have much secondary metabolites of medicinal importance. As Various adverse effect of synthetic drugs people are demanding natural drugs for safety in recent years. Through various literature surveys, we found that herb have been implemented in various pharmacological actions for development of drugs. The following research suggested that *Eleutherococcus senticosus* has significant bioactive compound and can be used for pharmacological studies and will make way for the production of herbal medicines for various ailments including genital herpes and type-2 diabetes.

Acknowledgement

The author thanks DST-FIST laboratory, DBT Star Scheme, chairman and managing Trustee of Dr. N.G.P Arts and Science College, Coimbatore, Tamil Nadu for providing necessary facilities for write this chapter.

5. Reference

1) Arouca, A and Grassi Kassisse, D. M. (2013). *Eleutherococcus senticosus*: studies and effects. *Health,* 5(9): 1509 - 1515.
2) Baczek, K. (2009). Accumulation of biologically active compounds in Eleuthero (*Eleutherococcus senticosus*/Rupr. et Maxim./Maxim.) grown in Poland. *Herba Polonica*, 55: 7 - 13.
3) Barkan, A. I., Gaiduchenia, L. I., and Makarenko, I. A. (1980). Effect of *Eleutherococcus* on respiratory viral infectious morbidity in children in organized collectives. *Pediatriia*, 4: 65 - 66.
4) Chen, M., Song, F., Guo, M., Liu, Z. and Liu, S. (2002). Analysis of flavonoid constituents from leaves of *Acanthopanax senticosus* Harms by electrospray tandem mass spectrometry. *Rapid Communications in Mass Spectrometry,* 16(4): 264 - 271.
5) Glatthaar Saalmüller, B., Sacher, F. and Esperester, A. (2001). Antiviral activity of an extract derived from roots of *Eleutherococcus senticosus. Antiviral Research*, 12(4): 1111 – 1119.
6) Huang, D. B., Ran, R. Z and Yu, Z. F. (2005). Effect of *Acanthopanax senticosus* injection on the activities of human Tumour necrosis factor and natural killer cell in blood in the patients with lung cancer. *Zhongguo Zhong Yao Za Zhi*, 30(8): 621 - 624.
7) Jin, L., Wu, F and Li, X. (2013) Anti-depressant effects of aqueous extract from *Acanthopanax senticosus* in mice. *Phytotherapy Research,* 27(12): 1829 – 1833.
8) Jung, C. H., Jung, H., Shin, Y. C., Park, J. H., Jun, C. Y., Kim, H. M., Yim, H. S., Shin, M. G., Bae, H. S., Kim, S. H., and Ko, S. G. (2007). *Eleutherococcus senticosus* extract attenuates LPS-induced iNOS expression through the inhibition of Akt and JNK pathways in murine macrophage. *Journal of Ethnopharmacology*, 113(1): 183 - 187.
9) Lee, J. M., Lee, D. G., Kim, J. and Lee, S. (2014). Content analysis of flavonoids in the stems and roots of *Acanthopanax* species in different countries. *Asian Journal of Chemistry,* 26(12): 3511 - 3514.
10) Miho Hatanaka, RDN, L.D. by Medically reviewed — Written by Jennifer Huizen on August 23, 2017.

11) Panossian, A., Wikman, G and Wagner, H. (1999). Plant adaptogens III. Earlier and more recent aspects and concepts on their mode of action. *Phytomedicine,* 6(4): 287 - 300.
12) Schmidt, M., Thomsen, M., Kelber O and Kraft, K. (2014). Myths and facts in herbal medicines: *Eleutherococcus senticosus* (*Siberian ginseng*) and its contraindication in hypertensive patients. *Botanics: Targets and Therapy,* 4: 27 – 32.
13) Verpoorte, R. (2000). Pharmacognosy in the new millennium: lead finding and biotechnology. *Journal of Pharmacy and Pharmacology,* 52(3): 253 - 262.
14) Watson, D H. (2003). Performance Functional Foods. Cambridge, UK: Woodhead (Woodhead Publishing in Food Science and Technology).
15) Yang, J., Zhao, S., Yu, C and Li, C. (2013) Large-scale plantlet conversion and *ex vitro* transplantation efficiency of *Siberian ginseng* by bioreactor culture. *The Scientific World Journal,* 13: 8 - 15.
16) Załuski, D., Smolarz, H. D and Gawlik-Dziki, U. (2012). Bioactive compounds and antioxidative, antileukemic and anti-MMPs activity of *Eleutherococcus* species cultivated in Poland. *Natural Product Communications,* 7(11): 1483 – 1486.
17) Załuski, D., Mendyk, E and Smolarz, H. D. (2016). Identification of MMP-1 and MMP-9 inhibitors from the roots of *Eleutherococcus divaricatus*, and the PAMPA test. *Natural Product Research,* 30(5): 595 – 599.

Advances in Pharmaceutical Sciences
ISBN: 978-81-951323-7-9
First Edition; Volume – 1; 2021
Chapter – 7, Page: 67 - 76

7

PHARMACOLOGICAL BENEFITS OF Citrus maxima (BURM.) MERR (POMELO) FRUIT JUICE

Fathima Nadeer* **and Jiby Abraham**

Department of Home Science (Nutrition & Dietetics), St Joseph's College for Women, Alappuzha – 688 001, Kerala, India.

*Corresponding author: fathimabidz@gmail.com; jibyabrahams24@gmail.com

Abstract

Citrus fruit such as Pomelo are considered under-utilized. The present study was carried out to study the effect of vitamin C and antioxidant content of Pomelo (Red and white variety) juices extracted by different juicing methods. Vitamin C analysis was done by Iodometric Titration. Total antioxidant activity of the juices were estimated by DPPH method. It was found that Vitamin C content in cold pressed juice was the highest and decreased in order manually squeezed and blender respectively. Manually squeezed pomelo white variety showed highest antioxidant activity. Pomelo which is an underutilised fruit with all the health benefits can be promoted for developing novel products from them.

Key words: Citrus fruit, Pomelo, Vitamin C, Antioxidant activity, DPPH method, Pharmacological activity and Fruit juice.

1. Introduction

The term "Citrus" belongs to the Rutaceae family refers to genus of flowering plants. Extensive list of Citrus hybrids and cultivars is available, mostly based on *Citrus maxima, Citrus medica,* and *Citrus reticulata* (Mandalari *et al.,* 2017).These are mostly consumed worldwide as fresh produce and juice. Citrus is one amongst the largest plant species that consists of forty or more varieties which are distributed worldwide. Citrus is one of the foremost vital fruits, which is consumed principally fresh and has been used as a flavouring, medication, additive or food supplement. Citrus is believed to possess bioactivities like antioxidant, anti-inflammatory, antimicrobial, and is usually recommended to be beneficial for cancer and chronic diseases (Karimi *et al.,* 2012). Commonly the peel is rejected as waste that contains a variety of secondary components with significant antioxidant activity when compared with other parts of the Citrus fruit. A number of studies have recognized the presence of polyphenols, vitamins, minerals, dietary fibres, essential oils and carotenoids content which makes citrus a health benefit promoting fruit .There is a growing acceptance that phenols, amino acids, essential oils, pectin, carotenoids, flavonoids, and vitamin C present in citrus fruits exert beneficial effects in the prevention of degenerative diseases .Vitamin C, phenolic and antioxidant activities of citrus fruits plays a great role in the concentration of flavanones which is greater in citrus albedo and the levels of flavones and flavonols vary in the flavedo and juice sacs.

Citrus maxima, a citrus variety usually referred to as "pomelo" is a common fruit wide fully grown and consumed fresh or processed into juice. It is a tropical plant species which originated from Southeast Asia and are widely cultivated in some parts of West Africa. *Citrus maxima* have two parts; the peel and pulp which can be easily separated out. The pulp is light coloured or pink and coarse with large, spindle-shaped juice sacks (Ani and Abel, 2018b). Citrus juices are consumed in large-scale which is mainly due to their biological process and special flavour. Lifestyle changes and raised awareness among health-conscious consumers have driven the beverage industry to develop and introduce purposeful drinks with additional nutritional values and health-promoting benefits. Moreover, the invasive demand for freshly squeezed un-pasteurised fruit and vegetable juices reflects changes in client preferences for beverages which does not undergo processing. Regular fruit juices are extracted by centrifugal juicers that utilize a fast-spinning metal blade close against a mesh filter. This method separates the juice extract from fruit flesh by centrifugal force. once the metal blade spins at a relatively high speed, it generates heat, which may negatively have an effect on the bio-active compound present in the fruit juice. Cold-pressed juices are extracted by cold-pressed extractors that initial crush then press the fruit to extract its juice at a very low speed. This extraction method generates nearly no heat and preserves the nutritional quality of the fruit juice. Cold pressed juice can help in reducing the stress of detoxification on the body. These juices are loaded with nutrients that aid in fighting toxins and boosting immunity and health. Cold pressed juice is so potent and instantaneous because it removes the fiber of the whole fruits. Body do not need to break the fiber down in the digestive system before it is to be used, cold pressed juice is like a kick start to the whole system. The nutrients immediately enter the body and starts its work. Fruit juice consumption is beneficial for the upkeep of better health and hindrance of diseases. The positive health advantages of juices have been ascribed partially to vitamin C (ascorbic acid), the most important vitamin found in fruits and vegetables (Hafid Boudries, 2012) .

2. Underutilised fruits in India

These species were rendered "Underutilized" by the fact that even though they are locally abundant, they are restricted to their geographical location with dearth of scientific knowledge about them, and their current use is linked to their economic potential. These species were immensely constructive by surviving harsh agro-climatic conditions, and can be established on degraded lands, which are presently being underutilized either due to poor soil fertility or moisture scarcity. Due to unsustainable market pressures and rapid urbanization, majority of these species have come to near extinction. India is the main centre of origin for many tropical fruit tree species, which are not commercially cultivated. It provides significant source of livelihood and support for many rural tribes. The tribal inhabitants of Western Ghats, Maharashtra and North Eastern States of India were traditionally reliant on non-timber forest products and favoured local fruit species like tamarind (*Tamarindus indica*), jackfruit (*Artocarpus heterophyllus*), Indian gooseberry (*Emblica officinalis*), ber (*Zizyphus mauritiana*), etc., instead of arable food crops apart from mango and cashew, for establishing agri-horti-forestry for their livelihoods. Innumerable wild species of Citrus, Musa, Pyrus and Malus were also prevalent in the North Eastern regions. Conversely, most of these species are in a state of neglect, while a trivial number of them are under cultivation in their native tracts by local communities for specific household uses only (Diengngan, 2015).

3. Citrus maxima (burm.) merr Fruit (Pomelo)

A citrus variety commonly known as Pomelo also called shaddock with its scientific name "*Citrus maxima* (Brum.) Merr" is a popular fruit which is underutilised (Sirisomboon and Lapchareonsuk, 2012). Pomelo is now being popular in Southeast Asia and worldwide which is one of the five most broadly cultivated and consumed citrus fruits, along with orange, mandarin, lemon, and grapefruit. Pomelo fruit weighs about 1 - 2 kg and attains a width of about 10 - 30 cm. Pomelo peel which make up 30 % of fresh fruit weight is considered largest and thickest when compared to other citrus fruit (Fazelin *et al.*, 2014). The flesh of pomelo contains important nutrients including vitamin C, para-insulin, potassium, pectin, natural folic acid and chromium. The pomelo fruit has a thin flavedo and thick albedo that protects the pomelo flesh from applied forces and evaporation of water and also helps in preventing damage during transportation. The flavedo and albedo of pomelos are rich in antioxidants. Phenolics present in flavedo are naringenin, hesperetin, diosmin, and gallic acid and hesperetin, diosmin, rutin, chlorogenic acid, and gallic acid are found in the albedo (Wang *et al.*, 2019). Pomelo fruits contains high amount of macronutrient in both the pulp and peel (Czech *et al.*, 2011).

4. Vitamin C and Anti-oxidant activity of Pomelo

Free radicals play an important part in pathogenesis of diseases which include rheumatoid arthritis, diabetes, cancer, and certain neurodegenerative, and pulmonary diseases. Antioxidants from natural products with antioxidant property help protect body against free radicals and are important in diet for obtaining and preserving good health (Mäkynen *et al.*, 2013). Fundamental functions of body such as growth, maintenance of health and metabolism are maintained by vitamins. Citrus fruits are rich source of antioxidants, which contain appreciable amount of ascorbic acid, flavonoids, and phenolic compounds (Sir Elkhatim *et al.*, 2018). Vitamin C in citrus fruits are important antioxidants that neutralize the effects of free radicals and will help prevent disease (Mditshwa *et al.,* 2017; Ani and Abel, 2018a). Antioxidant capacity of pomelo fruit are not mainly due to the phenolic compounds, but by ascorbic acid content in fruit. Vitamin C components of citrus fruits are said to counteract the cell infection by SARS-CoV-2, and modulate the systemic immunopathological phases of the condition (Bellavite and Donzelli, 2020).

5. Therapeutic Benefits of Pomelo

Citrus the prominent world fruit crops, accommodate active phytochemicals that protects health. Also, it provide sufficient supply of vitamin C, folic acid, potassium and pectin (Rafiq *et al.*, 2018).Citrus fruit is said to have synergistic or antagonistic effects(Turner and Burri, 2013). Pomelo pulp has been used in the past as an appetizer, antitoxic, cardiac stimulant, and stomach tonic. Flavonoids mainly present in pomelo are neo-hesperidin, hesperidin, naringenin, and naringin, mainly found in appreciable amount in fruit juices. Natural flavonoids aid in prevention of diabetic complications as they are capable of affecting multiple mechanisms in the inhibition of glycation (Caengprasath *et al.*, 2013).The antioxidant constituents of citrus fruits, such as ascorbic acid and flavonoids which are antioxidant constituents present in citrus fruits helps in scavenging Reactive Oxygen Species (ROS) and will help prevent ROS accumulation and oxidative damage. Pomelo fruit contribute in endothelial wound closure and cell migration (Buachan *et al.*, 2014). Citrus peels are abundant with flavonoid hesperidin which was found to be helpful in fighting against COVID-19 (Meneguzzo *et al.*, 2020). Pomelo leaf extract is found to exhibit hepatoprotective, hypolipidemic, anti-inflammatory and antioxidant activities which will probably be due to the presence of phenolic compounds (Feksa *et al.*, 2018). Citrus peel plays a role in lowering the plasma liver cholesterol, serum triglyceride level, serum total cholesterol, liver total lipids, and liver cholesterol as suggested in certain epidemiological studies (Rafiq *et al.,* 2018). Pomelo peel powder is said to have a preventive effect on CCl4 induced liver injury (Chowdhury *et al.*, 2015). Flavonoids present in *Citrus maxima* imparts anticancer activity (Kundu Sen *et al.,* 2011). Pomelo peels contain bioactive compounds which shows numerous health benefits like antiatherogenic, anti-inflammatory, antitumor activity, anticlotting, antimicrobial, and antioxidant activity (Ani and Abel, 2018b). Pomelo fruit is used in indigenous medicine as sedative, for treatment of convulsive cough, haemorrhage and epilepsy (Vijaylakshmi and Radha, 2015). *Citrus maxima* leaf extract exhibited pharmacological properties and possess analgesic, anti-inflammatory, anti-tumour, hepatoprotective and CNS activity, Plant stem of pomelo shows anti-diabetic activity. Pomelo flesh exhibits hypocholesterolemic and anti-oxidant activity, Citrus maxima is a high value medicinal plant.

6. Cold-press juices

Citrus juices are widely consumed due to their nutritional benefits and variety of pharmacological properties (Bharate and Bharate, 2012). Cold-pressed juices have been introduced as a new generation of fruit beverages and are claimed by beverage manufacturers to retain higher levels of antioxidants and bioactive compounds when compared with other juicing methods (Khaksar *et al.*, 2017). Cold-pressed juices is also said to have a longer shelf life than other methods. Cold-pressed juices retain lot of nutrients which aid in destroying toxins and help boost health and immunity. Juice extracted by cold pressed method lacks fibre by which the nutrients immediately enters the body and will overcome the strenuous job of digestive system to break down fibre(Franklin, 2018)and making digestion easier. Cold Pressing retains the taste and quality of the fresh fruit which is not possible in heat and chemical pasteurization it also kills bacteria on a structural level (Kent, 2019). The increased demand of processed citrus i.e. citrus juice provides impetuson citrus juice manufacturers to maintain the quality of juiceto maintain original nutritional value of citrus fruits (Bharate and Bharate, 2012).

7. Vitamin C

Pomelo (Red & White Var) was juiced by different juicing methods like cold pressing, manual squeezing and in blender. Vitamin C content of pomelo juice was estimated by Iodometric titration method. The method involved in iodometric titration is the reaction of iodine with ascorbic acid, which oxidizes it to dehydroascorbic acid. The endpoint of redox titration is determined by the first iodine in increased amount that is complexed with starch, giving a deep blue-violet colour (Silva *et al.,* 1999). The content of Vitamin C in Cold-pressed juice was the highest and was lower in manually squeezed and blenderized juices. The lower contents in Blender juice are mainly due to the thermolysis and oxidation of Vitamin C, after blending with high-speed rotating blades (Khaksar *et al.*, 2017; Kim *et al.*, 2017). On comparing the nutritional value of grape juice was compared by using different juicers: low-speed masticating juicer, high-speed centrifugal juicer, and a blender. It was investigated that the juice extracted from a low-speed masticating juicer had a higher nutritional quality than the other types. Vitamin C is an essential nutrient which is not synthesized by human body due to loss of a key enzyme in the biosynthetic pathway. It also takes part in collagen synthesis in order to prevent scurvy and other vitamin C related deficiency diseases. It is an excellent antioxidant to scavenge free radicals and to prevent oxidative stress (Hai Liu, 2013).

8. Anti-oxidant activity

DPPH (2,2-diphenyl-1-picryl-hydrazyl-hydrate) is a free radical based antioxidant assay on electron-transfer which produces a violet-coloured solution in ethanol. It also provide an easy and rapid way to determine the antioxidant activity (Garcia *et al.*, 2012). Antioxidant capacity has been used widely as a tool to evaluate the quality of fruit juices after processing and during storage (Khaksar *et al.*, 2017). A high antioxidant activity in manually squeezed pomelo juice as this method generates no heat and preserves the nutritional quality of the juice. In a comparative study red-fleshed pomelo juice had a higher content of lycopene, β-carotene, soluble protein, and soluble solid, and also depicted a stronger (DPPH)-radical scavenging activity, reducing power activity and bile-acid-binding activity, as well as higher anti-proliferative activity in cancer cells, High amounts of lycopene and β-carotene in the red-fleshed pomelo fruits will be a lead to high antioxidant, hypolipidemic and anticancer property. Hence, red pomelo juice will be a potential natural resource for multitargeted pharmacological and oncological therapies (Qiu *et al.*, 2020).

9. Conclusion and Perspectives

Citrus consumption has tremendous health benefits. Citrus fruits are nutrient-dense foods that can be good sources of carbohydrates, including dietary fibre, and many vitamins and minerals. Citrus fruits are equally valuable among populations who need to overcome and prevent micronutrient deficiencies as well as those concerned with problems of over-nutrition, obesity and diet-related chronic diseases. Though minor fruits are popularly known as 'less known fruits' these fruits have great values both in nutritional and medicinal properties. *Citrus maxima* which is an underutilized fruit which is unrecognized without considering its nutritive properties and health benefits, Pomelo fruit can be utilized effectively by developing novel products that will have good health benefits as well as having therapeutic potential in terms of significant antioxidant activity and vitamin C content which will thereby increase the demand of the fruit. Red variety Pomelo was found to be superior in therapeutic effects and acceptability. Pomelo can be exploited in terms of nutrients and health supplements for their potential use in food industry.

10. References

1) Ani, P. N., & Abel, H. C. (2018a). Nutrient, phytochemical, and antinutrient composition of Citrus maxima fruit juice and peel extract. *Food Science and Nutrition*, *6*(3). https://doi.org/10.1002/fsn3.604
2) Ani, P. N., & Abel, H. C. (2018b). Nutrient, phytochemical, and antinutrient composition of Citrus maxima fruit juice and peel extract. *Food Science and Nutrition*, *6*(3), 653–658. https://doi.org/10.1002/fsn3.604
3) Bellavite, P., & Donzelli, A. (2020). Hesperidin and SARS-CoV-2: New light on the healthy function of citrus fruits. In *Antioxidants* (Vol. 9, Issue 8). https://doi.org/10.3390/antiox9080742
4) Bharate, S. S., & Bharate, S. B. (2012). *Non-enzymatic browning in citrus juice: chemical markers, their detection and ways to improve product quality*. https://doi.org/10.1007/s13197-012-0718-8
5) Buachan, P., Chularojmontri, L., & Wattanapitayakul, S. K. (2014). Selected Activities of Citrus Maxima Merr. Fruits on Human Endothelial Cells: Enhancing Cell Migration and Delaying Cellular Aging. *Nutrients*, *6*, 1618–1634. https://doi.org/10.3390/nu6041618
6) Caengprasath, N., Ngamukote, S., Mäkynen, K., & Adisakwattana, S. (2013). The protective effects of pomelo extract (Citrus grandis L. Osbeck) against fructose-mediated protein oxidation and glycation. *EXCLI Journal*, *12*, 491–502. http://www.ncbi.nlm.nih.gov/pubmed/26966424

7) Chowdhury, M. R. H., Sagor, M. A. T., Tabassum, N., Potol, M. A., Hossain, H., & Alam, M. A. (2015). Supplementation of Citrus maxima Peel Powder Prevented Oxidative Stress, Fibrosis, and Hepatic Damage in Carbon Tetrachloride (CCl4) Treated Rats. *Evidence-Based Complementary and Alternative Medicine, 2015.* https://doi.org/10.1155/2015/598179
8) Czech, A., Zarycka, E., Yanovych, D., Zasadna, Z., Grzegorczyk, I., & Kłys, S. (2011). *Mineral Content of the Pulp and Peel of Various Citrus Fruit Cultivars.* https://doi.org/10.1007/s12011-019-01727-1
9) Diengngan S, H. M. (2015). Genetic Diversity of Underutilized Fruits in India for Environmental Sustainability. *Advances in Plants & Agriculture Research*, *2*(7). https://doi.org/10.15406/apar.2015.02.00076
10) Fazelin, N., Zain, M., Yusop, S. M., & Ahmad, I. (2014). Preparation and Characterization of Cellulose and Nanocellulose From Pomelo (Citrus grandis) Albedo. *J Nutr Food Sci*, *5*, 1. https://doi.org/10.4172/2155-9600.1000334
11) Feksa, D. L., Coelho, R. P., Aparecida da Costa Güllich, A., Dal Ponte, E. S., da Costa Escobar Piccoli, J., & Manfredini, V. (2018). Extract of Citrus maxima (pummelo) leaves improve hepatoprotective activity in Wistar rats submitted to the induction of non-alcoholic hepatic steatosis. *Biomedicine and Pharmacotherapy*, *98*, 338–346. https://doi.org/10.1016/j.biopha.2017.12.070
12) Franklin, R. (2018). *The Wonderful Benefits of Cold Pressed Juice — Pure Green Juice and Smoothies.* https://www.puregreen.com/pure-green-magazine/benefits-of-cold-pressed-juice/
13) Garcia, E. J., Cadorin Oldoni, T. L., de Alencar, S. M., Reis, A., Loguercio, A. D., &Miranda Grande, R. H. (2012). Antioxidant activity by DPPH assay of potential solutions to be applied on bleached teeth. *Brazilian Dental Journal*, *23*(1). https://doi.org/10.1590/S0103-64402012000100004
14) Hafid Boudries. (2012). Pulp antioxidant activities, mineral contents and juice nutritional properties of Algerian Clementine Cultivars and Mandarin. *AFRICAN JOURNAL OF BIOTECHNOLOGY*, *11*(18). https://doi.org/10.5897/ajb11.2943
15) Hai Liu, R. (2013). *Supplement White Vegetables: A Forgotten Source of Nutrients Health-Promoting Components of Fruits and Vegetables in the Diet 1,2. 4*, 384–392. https://doi.org/10.3945/an.112.003517
16) Karimi, E., Oskoueian, E., Hendra, R., Oskoueian, A., & Jaafar, H. Z. E. (2012). Phenolic Compounds Characterization and Biological Activities of Citrus aurantium Bloom. *Molecules*, *17*(2), 1203–1218. https://doi.org/10.3390/molecules17021203

17) Kent. (2019). *Benefits of Using Cold Pressed Juicer.* https://www.kent.co.in/blog/health-benefits-of-using-a-cold-pressed-juicer/
18) Khaksar, G., Assatarakul, K., & Sirikantaramas, S. (2017). *Effect of cold-pressed and normal centrifugal juicing on quality attributes of fresh juices: do cold-pressed juices harbor a superior nutritional quality and antioxidant capacity?* https://doi.org/10.1016/j.heliyon.2019.e01917
19) Kim, M. J., Jun, J. G., Park, S. Y., Choi, M. J., Park, E., Kim, J. I., & Kim, M. J. (2017). Antioxidant activities of fresh grape juices prepared using various household processing methods. *Food Science and Biotechnology*, *26*(4), 861–869. https://doi.org/10.1007/s10068-017-0120-4
20) KunduSen, S., Gupta, M., Mazumder, U. K., Haldar, P. K., Saha, P., & Bala, A. (2011). Antitumor Activity of Citrus maxima (Burm.) Merr. Leaves in Ehrlich's Ascites Carcinoma Cell-Treated Mice . *ISRN Pharmacology*, *2011*, 1–4. https://doi.org/10.5402/2011/138737
21) Mäkynen, K., Jitsaardkul, S., Tachasamran, P., Sakai, N., Puranachoti, S., Nirojsinlapachai, N., Chattapat, V., Caengprasath, N., Ngamukote, S., & Adisakwattana, S. (2013). Cultivar variations in antioxidant and antihyperlipidemic properties of pomelo pulp (Citrus grandis [L.] Osbeck) in Thailand. *Food Chemistry*, *139*(1–4). https://doi.org/10.1016/j.foodchem.2013.02.017
22) Mandalari, G., Bisignano, C., Cirmi, S., & Navarra, M. (2017). *Effectiveness of Citrus Fruits on Helicobacter pylori*. https://doi.org/10.1155/2017/8379262
23) Mditshwa, A., Magwaza, L. S., Tesfay, S. Z., & Opara, U. L. (2017). Postharvest factors affecting vitamin C content of citrus fruits: A review. In *Scientia Horticulturae* (Vol. 218, pp. 95–104). Elsevier B.V. https://doi.org/10.1016/j.scienta.2017.02.024
24) Meneguzzo, F., Ciriminna, R., Zabini, F., & Pagliaro, M. (2020). Review of evidence available on hesperidin-rich products as potential tools against COVID-19 and hydrodynamic cavitation-based extraction as a method of increasing their production. In *Processes* (Vol. 8, Issue 5). https://doi.org/10.3390/PR8050549
25) Qiu, D., Yang, H., Li, M., Kui, X., Sun, Y., & Li, J.-A. (2020). Comparative Studies on the Quality and Lycopene Content of Pomelo (Citrus grandis Osbeck) Cultivars. In *Natural Product Communications* (Vol. 15, Issue 9).
26) Rafiq, S., Kaul, R., Sofi, S. A., Bashir, N., Nazir, F., & Ahmad Nayik, G. (2018). Citrus peel as a source of functional ingredient: A review. In *Journal of the Saudi Society of Agricultural Sciences* (Vol. 17, Issue 4). https://doi.org/10.1016/j.jssas.2016.07.006

27) Silva, C. R., Simoni, J. A., Collins, C. H., & Volpe, P. L. O. (1999). Ascorbic Acid as a Standard for Iodometric Titrations: An Analytical Experiment for General Chemistry. *Journal of Chemical Education*, *76*(10), 1421–1422. https://doi.org/10.1021/ed076p1421

28) Sir Elkhatim, K. A., Elagib, R. A. A., & Hassan, A. B. (2018). Content of phenolic compounds and vitamin C and antioxidant activity in wasted parts of Sudanese citrus fruits. *Food Science and Nutrition*, *6*(5), 1214–1219. https://doi.org/10.1002/fsn3.660

29) Sirisomboon, P., & Lapchareonsuk, R. (2012). *Evaluation of the physicochemical and textural properties of pomelo fruit following storage. Evaluation of the physicochemical and textural properties of pomelo fruit following storage*. *67*(6), 399–413. https://doi.org/10.1051/fruits/2012034

30) Turner, T., & Burri, B. (2013). Potential Nutritional Benefits of Current Citrus Consumption. *Agriculture*, *3*(1), 170–187. https://doi.org/10.3390/agriculture3010170

31) Vijaylakshmi, P., & Radha, R. (2015). An overview: Citrus maxima. *The Journal of Phytopharmacology*, *4*(5), 263–267. www.phytopharmajournal.com

32) Wang, F., Lin, J., Xu, L., Peng, Q., Huang, H., Tong, L., Lu, Q., Wang, C., & Yang, L. (2019). On higher nutritional and medical properties of a carotenoid-rich mutant pomelo (Citrus maxima (L.) Osbeck). *Industrial Crops and Products*, *127*. https://doi.org/10.1016/j.indcrop.2018.10.065

Advances in Pharmaceutical Sciences
ISBN: 978-81-951323-7-9
First Edition; Volume – 1; 2021
Chapter – 8, Page: 77 - 83

8

GENERAL PROPERTIES AND PHARMACOLOGICAL BENEFITS OF *Syzygium jambos*

Devakumar Joseph* and Sudha Sivasubramanian

PG & Research Department of Microbiology, Dr. N.G.P. Arts and Science College, Coimbatore-641 048, Tamil Nadu, India.

*Corresponding author: devakumar09@gmail.com

Abstract

Jambos is an evergreen tree with a regular shaped, dense crown of wide-spreading branches, it can row 6 - 10 metres tall. An attractive tree with showy cream-coloured flowers and dark-green foliage, is often grown as an ornamental and hedge plant in tropical gardens. The genus is native to India, laysia, Myanmar, Philippines, Sri Lanka, Bangladesh, Pakistan, Guangdong, Guangxi and land. Fruit - usually eaten raw, the fruit can also be stewed, made into jams, jellies, confections veral parts of the tree are used medicinally as a tonic or a diuretic. In India, the fruit is regarded ic for the brain and liver. The leaf decoction is applied to sore eyes, also serves as a diuretic ctorant and treatment for rheumatism. The *Syzygium jambos* (Rose apple) fruits have wide medicinal properties to human being like control diabetes, reduce toxicity and boosts stem etc. Plants develop massive root systems and can be useful for stabilizing soils on With the above information the plant *Syzygium jambos* have significant medicinal inst bacterial and fungal infections as well as drug candidate for non-communicable

s, Rose apple, Medicinal properties and *Syzygium jambos*.

1. Introduction

Jambos is an evergreen tree with a regular shaped, dense crown of wide-spreading branches, it can grow 6 - 10 metres tall. The bole can be 50cm in diameter, often branching from low down (Figure 1). A multipurpose tree that has been cultivated for around 2,500 years. It provides food, medicines and a range of commodities for the local population. An attractive tree with showy cream-coloured flowers and dark-green foliage, it is often grown as an ornamental and hedge plant in tropical gardens. It is also sometimes cultivated for its Edible fruit (Chittenden, 1951).

Figure – 1: *Syzygium jambos* – Tree, Flower and Fruits

The edible fruit of *Syzygium jambos* is shaped like some kinds of guava; in fact, the fruit is so like the guava in appearance that people unfamiliar with it may mistake it for a guava on sight. However, the fragrance, flavour and texture are different, and instead of containing dozens of small, hard seeds set in a jelly-like tissue, as a guava does, the fruit of *Syzygium jambos* usually contains one or two large, unarmoured seeds about a cm in diameter, lying loose in a slightly fluffy cavity when ripe. Shaking a fruit to feel whether the seeds rattle, gives some indication whether it is ripe. The skin is thin and waxy. The flowers are described by some as fragrant, though this appears to be a variable attribute. The ripe fruit, however, has a strong, pleasant floral bouquet, hence such common names as "Rose apple" and "pomarrosa" (Hargreaves *et al.,* 1964).

2. Common Names

Syzygium jambos has several common names, reflecting the large number of regions in which it occurs as a garden or fruit tree or as an invader. The names include *Guljamun* , *madhura nelli*, Malabar Plum, *Panineer Champakka*, *Mountain Apple (champoo), chom pu* or *chom-phu*. Terms like "plum rose", "water apple", "Cloud apple", "Wax apple", "Malay apple", "jambrosade", "PauTêe"(Penang Hokkien spelled with Taiwanese Romanisation System), "pomarrosa", or the English equivalent, "rose apple". Several of these names also are applied to other species of *Syzygium*, while *"jambu"* can also mean a guava. In Bangla, the fruit is called "golap-jaam". In Karnataka the English common name is "rose apple", and the vernacular name is Pannerale (Paneer hannu), while the name for the other one is Nerale.

3. Geographic Distribution

The genus is native to India, Malaysia, Myanmar, Philippines, Sri Lanka, Bangladesh, Pakistan, Guangdong, Guangxi and Thailand. It is considered as exotic in Algeria, Antigua, Barbuda, Australia, Bahamas, Barbados, Colombia, Cuba, Dominica, Ghana, Grenada, Guadeloupe, Guatemala, Guyana, Jamaica, Kenya, Martinique, Mexico, Montserrat, Nepal, Netherlands Antilles, Nicaragua, Panama, South Africa, St Kitts and Nevis, St Lucia, St Vincent and the Grenadines, Sudan, Tanzania, Trinidad and United States of America (Panggabean, 1991; Venkata Ratnam, 2008).

4. Edible Uses

Fruit - usually eaten raw, the fruit can also be stewed, made into jams, jellies, confections etc. A sweet flavour with a crisp and crunchy texture, the fruit is somewhat to very juicy and has a delicate, rose-water fragrance. When cooked with custards or puddings, they impart a rose-like flavour. The large, hollow seed cavity is sometimes utilized to stuff the fruits and bake them. The fruit has to be handled very carefully after harvesting because it bruises easily and then loses its crispness. The fruit is up to 4 cm x 6 cm, around the tropical world, the fruit is mostly eaten out-of-hand by children. It is seldom marketed. In the home, it is sometimes stewed with some sugar and served as dessert. The fruit can be distilled to yield a rosewater that is said to be equal to the best obtained from rose petals (Huxley 1992).

5. Medicinal Uses

Several parts of the tree are used medicinally as a tonic or a diuretic. In India, the fruit is regarded as a tonic for the brain and liver. An infusion of the fruit acts as a diuretic. A sweetened preparation of the flowers is believed to reduce fever. The seeds are employed against diarrhoea, dysentery and catarrh. In Nicaragua, it has been claimed that an infusion of roasted, powdered seeds is beneficial to diabetics. They say in Colombia that the seeds have an anaesthetic property. The leaf decoction is applied to sore eyes, also serves as a diuretic and expectorant and treatment for rheumatism. The juice of macerated leaves is taken as a febrifuge. Powdered leaves have been rubbed on the bodies of smallpox patients for the cooling effect. The bark contains 7 - 12.4 % tannin. It is astringent, emetic and cathartic. The decoction is administered to relieve asthma, bronchitis and hoarseness. Cuban people believe that the root is an effective remedy for epilepsy (Manandhar, 2002; Suranant, 2001).

Several parts of the tree are used medicinally as a tonic or a diuretic. In India, the fruit is regarded as a tonic for the brain and liver. An infusion of the fruit acts as a diuretic. A sweetened preparation of the flowers is believed to reduce fever. The seeds are employed against diarrhoea, dysentery and catarrh. In Nicaragua, it has been claimed that an infusion of roasted, powdered seeds is beneficial to diabetics. They say in Colombia that the seeds have an anaesthetic property. The leaf decoction is applied to sore eyes, also serves as a diuretic and expectorant and treatment for rheumatism. The juice of macerated leaves is taken as a febrifuge. Powdered leaves have been rubbed on the bodies of smallpox patients for the cooling effect. The bark contains 7 - 12.4 % tannin. It is astringent, emetic and cathartic. The decoction is administered to relieve asthma, bronchitis and hoarseness. Cuban people believe that the root is an effective remedy for epilepsy (Manandhar 2002, Suranant, 2001).

6. Agroforestry Uses

Plants develop massive root systems and can be useful for stabilizing soils on river banks. However, the dense top growth can stop any plant growth underneath, and this has sometimes led to sheet erosion unless the crown is thinned. Bees produce a heavy, consistent flow of amber honey from the flowers (Francis 1990).

7. Benefits of *Syzygium jambos* fruit (Rose apple)

The *Syzygium jambos* (Rose apple) fruits have wide range of medicinal properties to human being like control diabetes, reduce toxicity and boosts immune system etc. (Figure – 2).

Figure – 2: General medicinal uses of *Syzygium jambos* fruits

Controls Diabetes

Rose apples contain Jambosine, an alkaloid type that can block or regulate the exchange of starch into sugar. This is essential for those people who are at risk of developing diabetes.

Helps in Digestion

The high fiber content present in rose apples makes it great for regulating the food passage through the digestive tract. This helps to relieve constipation and other health problems. In addition, the seeds of the rose apples have been used for preventing diarrhea and dysentery.

Prevents Cancer

Rose apples contain active organic compounds, together with Vitamin C and A. Early studies and traditional medical research proves prostate cancer and breast cancer is reducible with the addition of rose apples to your diet.

Reduces Toxicity

Rose apple decoction have been utilized as a diuretic substance for many years. This has been helpful in removing toxins from the liver and kidney while improving overall health and metabolism in our body.

Improves Heart Health

Rose apples contain fiber and nutrients that show positive effects on controlling cholesterol levels, reduce the risk of atherosclerosis, and prevent cardiovascular problems like strokes, heart disease, and heart attacks.

Boosts Immune System

Rose apples contain active and volatile compounds that have been connected with having anti-microbial and anti-fungal effects. Studies have proven that it can protect the skin from developing several infections and can improve immune system against various diseases.

Treats Bladder Infections

People suffering from bladder infections should include rose apples in their diet. The fruit contains chemical compounds that help in flushing out toxins. It is a natural diuretic which can stimulate the disposal of urine for people suffering from bladder problems. In addition, consuming rose apples can also help in preventing kidney stones formation.

Prevents Dehydration during Pregnancy

Pregnant women get dehydrated quite often as they get nauseous. During that period, drinking rose apple juice is an effective way to prevent dehydration. In addition, rose apples contain vitamins and minerals that are essential for pregnant women.

Strengthen Bones

Rose apples have strong calcium content to maintain bone health. A 100 gram serving of rose apples can provide 29 mg of calcium. Consuming this fruit daily can provide calcium requirement and make bones stronger.

Treats Coeliac Disease

People suffering from coeliac disease should consume rose apples daily. It is said to repair stomach lining that is damaged by coeliac disease.

Hydrates Skin

Rose apples hydrate and cleanses skin. You can apply the juice of rose apple on your face until it dries up. This can help in balancing the oil production and serve as a hydrating mask.

Promote Healthy Hair

Rose apples contain a compound known as procyanidin B-2 which stimulates hair growth and thickening. Using its extract can prevent hair thinning and baldness.

8. Conclusion

Medicinal plants are generally known and popular for a number of health benefits such as decreasing of blood pressure, prevention of cardiovascular diseases, or reducing the risk of cancer also due to their antioxidant activity because the plants hold numerous phytoconstituents. Equally, our plant *Syzygium jambos* also have significant medicinal properties against bacterial and fungal infections as well as drug candidate for non-communicable disease.

9. References

1) Chittenden Fred J. Ed., Royal Horticultural Society Dictionary of Gardening, Oxford (1951).
2) Francis JK. *Syzygium jambos* (L.) Alst. Rose apple. Myrtaceae. Myrtle family. USDA Forest Service, Southern Forest Experiment Station, Institute of Tropical Forestry (1990).
3) Hargreaves, Dorothy. Hargreaves, Bob. Tropical Trees of Hawaii. Kailua, Hawaii: Hargreaves. 54 (1964).
4) Huxley A. The New RHS Dictionary of Gardening. MacMillan Press (1992).
5) Manandhar. N. P. Plants and People of Nepal. Timber Press. Oregon (2002).
6) Panggabean G. Syzygium malaccense (L.). Plant Resources of South-East Asia 2: Edible Fruits and Nuts. Pudoc, Wageningen, the Netherlands.13: 292–294. 26 (1991).
7) Suranant Subhadrabandhu. Under-Utilized Tropical Fruits of Thailand. RAP Publication. F. A. O., The United Nations, Bangkok (2001).
8) Venkata Ratnam K and Venkata Raju RR. *In vitro* Antimicrobial Screening of the Fruit Extracts of Two *Syzygium* Species (Myrtaceae). Advances in Biol. Res. 2: 17-20 (2008).

Advances in Pharmaceutical Sciences
ISBN: 978-81-951323-7-9
First Edition; Volume – 1; 2021
Chapter – 9, Page: 84 - 95

9

PHARMACOLOGICAL ACTIVITIES OF SOME TERRESTRIAL PLANTS AND MARINE ALGAE

T. Ramesh[1], A. Amuthavalli[2] and T. Raajesh Kannan[3]

[1]PG & Research Department of Biotechnology, Hindustan College of Arts & Science, Kelambakkam, Tamil Nadu, India

[2]Mohamed Sathak Teacher Training College - B.Ed., Kelambakkam, Tamil Nadu, India

[3]Sri Muthukumaran College of Education, Chikkarayapuram, Chennai, Tamil Nadu, India

*Corresponding author: drrameshtbt@gmail.com

Abstract

The natural products derived from plants and marine algae have been used to treat human diseases. Traditional medicines have been practiced from time immemorial and have been well accepted and utilized by people throughout history. Natural medicinal products have drawn the attention of researchers around the world for many years due to their positive effects on human health and minimum side effects. Natural products are a repository of biologically active compounds with medicinal properties. In recent years, a considerable number of novel bioactive compounds with potent pharmacological properties have been isolated from natural products. Natural products such as plants, animals, microorganisms, and marine-based living organisms serve as the reservoir for many pharmacologically active compounds. More than two thousand biologically active compounds were isolated and characterized from plant-based materials. These bioactive compounds are potentially active against viruses, bacteria, fungi, and other human and animal diseases. Given that the present chapter aims at providing literature data of selective medicinally important terrestrial plants and marine algae available in the Indian subcontinent along with a critical review on its pharmacological activities.

Key words: Pharmacology, Plant-based medicine, Terrestrial plants and Marine algae.

1. Introduction

People have relied upon nature for their straightforward necessities just like the hotspots for prescriptions, covers, food stuffs, scents, clothing, flavors, manures and methods for transportation all through the ages. For the huge extents of total populace restorative plants keep on showing a prevailing job in the medical care framework and this is essentially evident in non-industrial nations, where natural medication has persistent history of long use. The turn of events and acknowledgment of restorative and monetary guides of these plants are on ascent in both industrialized and agricultural countries. The therapeutic potential of plant products may be traced back over 5,000 years, since evidence of their use in the treatment of ailments and for body system revitalization can be found in Indian and Egyptian civilizations (Bailey and Day, 1989; Mahesh and Satish 2008; Bamola *et al.,* 2018). In India, plants of therapeutic potential are broadly used by all sections of people. Both as folk medicines in numerous indigenous medical systems such as Ayurveda, Siddha, and Unani, and as processed pharmaceutical industrial products (Srinivasan *et al.,* 2007; Wijesekara *et al.,* 2011). Only about 500,000 plant species have been investigated phytochemically for biological or pharmacological activities in India's 4.5 million plant species (Singh and Kumar, 2017).

One of the most important sectors in the world is pharmaceuticals. It manufactures a variety of dosage forms such as tablets, capsules, solutions, syrups, suspensions, ointments, gels, creams, vaccines, and injections. Excipients and the active medicinal component are both present in a dose form (Guven *et al.,* 2010; Nishant, 2016). Any component that has pharmacological activity is considered an active medicinal ingredient. Excipients are inactive chemicals that are utilized to deliver medication as a medium or vehicle. The active ingredients' solubility, stability, and bioavailability can all be influenced by excipients (El-Gamal, 2010). Fillers, lubricants, colorants, antioxidants, preservatives, adjuvants, stabilizers, thickeners, emulsifiers, solubilizers, permeation enhancers, flavoring, and aromatic substances, as well as the outer covering of medicinal products, such as gelatin capsules, are all examples of excipients (Singh *et al.*, 2017).

2. Medicinally Important Plants

Medicinal and aromatic plants can help rural people, particularly women, improve their subsistence livelihoods in an environmentally friendly way while preserving the biodiversity of these natural resources (Sharma *et al.,* 2017). According to the World Health Organization (WHO), traditional medicine serves as the primary healthcare provider for up to 80 % of the World's population. The creation of indigenous medicines and the application of medicinal plants for the treatment of various diseases have significant economic benefits (Yadav *et al.,* 2017).

Individual and community health benefits greatly from medicinal plants. Plants have medical value due to chemical active compounds that have a defined physiological effect on the human body (Narendiran *et al.*, 2016). Plants are a rich source of bioactive compounds and could be used as a mosquito control agent in the future. Plant secondary metabolites, often known as phytochemicals, exhibit a wide range of pharmacological properties, including anti-oxidant, anti-allergic, antibacterial, hypoglycaemic, and anti-carcinogenic properties. These secondary metabolites protect cells from free radicals, which are unstable chemicals that cause cell harm (Harini and Nithyalakshmi, 2017). Natural antibacterial chemicals, particularly those produced from plants, are becoming increasingly popular for food preservation. As a result, there is a need to look for therapeutic herbs (Chavan, 2016).

Allium sativum Linn.

Alliin, Ajoene, and Flavonoids, are phytochemicals that extracted from fresh or crushed garlic. It used to treat many diseases (Augusti, 1996; Eidi *et al.,* 2006; Vinay Singh and Dinesh Singh, 2008).

Aloe vera

Aloe vera is used as a moisturizer and anti-irritant to prevent nasal chafing. *Aloe* extract used to prepare soaps, sunscreens, incense, shaving cream, and shampoos. It acts as astringent and it make body cool (Hamman, 2008; Rajeswari *et al.*, 2012; Priyanka Sharma *et al.*, 2014).

Carica papaya Linn.

The ripe fruit of the papaya contain phytochemicals such as polyphenols, carotenoids, benzyl isothiocyanates and benzyl glucosinates. Prunasin, a cyanogenic chemical found in papaya seeds. These chemicals used to cure many ailments (Mahendra *et al.,* 2016; Smita *et al.,* 2017; Priyadarshi and Ram, 2018; Sagadevan *et al.*, 2019).

Curcuma longa Linn.

Curcuma longa (Turmeric) has been utilized in Ayurvedic and Siddha treatments as a topically applied remedy for indigestion, throat infections, common colds, and liver diseases, as well as internally for indigestion, throat infections, common colds, and liver problems. It is a powerful antioxidant (Araújo and Leon, 2001; Goel *et al.,* 2008; Louay Labban, 2014; Rahul Kumar Verma *et al.*, 2018).

Mentha spicta Linn.

Mentha spicta is known for its fragrant oil, sometimes known as spearmint oil. Limonene, dihydrocarvone, and 1,8-cineol are all present in high proportions in spearmint oil (Sevindik, 2018; Mohammed Ali-Shtayeh *et al.*, 2019). Spearmint essential oil is an excellent insecticide against adult moths when used as a fumigant (Li and Tian, 2018; Tafrihi *et al.*, 2021).

3. Medicinally Important Marine Algae

Marine algae have a variety of components with potential health advantages, including several that are heavy metal chelators. Marine macro-algae is a primitive type of plant that lacks true roots, stems, and leaves, and has been classified into Phaeophyta (Brown), Rhodophyta (Red), and Chlorophyta (Green) types 6 depending on pigmentation (Nwosu *et al.*, 2011; Wang *et al.,* 2014; McHugh, 2003; Anon, 2005).

Poly-Unsaturated Fatty Acids (PUFAs), sterols, proteins, polysaccharides, antioxidants, and pigments are among the many physiologically active substances found in marine algae. They have a substantially higher concentration of over 60 trace elements than terrestrial plants. Protein, iodine, bromine, vitamins, stimulatory and antibacterial chemicals are also present (Sahoo *et al.,* 2003; Ravindran, Thangaradjou and Kannan, 2004, Muthuvelan *et al.*, 2001; Abou-Elela *et al.*, 2009; Mohammed *et al.*, 2007).

Padina boergesenii

Senthilkumar *et al.* (2014) found that *Padina boergesenii*, brown algae abundantly thriving in the Gulf of Mannar, Tamil Nadu, India, has antidiabetic activity, antioxidant activity, hepatoprotective activity, chemo-preventive effects, and herbivory effects (Vasanthi *et al.*, 2003; Guillermo *et al.,* 2007; Pandit *et al.,* 2010; Rajamani *et al.,* 2010).

Gracilaria edulis

Koneri *et al.* (2018) investigated the anti-diabetic effects of marine species in diabetic rats caused by STZ. The marine algae were collected from the off coast of Mandapam in the Gulf of Manner, Tamil Nadu. Carbohydrates, glycosides, phytosterol, proteins, and phytosterol were the main bioactive phytochemicals found. Methanolic extract of *Gracilaria edulis* significantly normalized all of the lipid abnormalities associated with diabetes and this algae also revealed a considerable rise in beta cell density, indicating property insulin secretohoge activity, which could be attributed to beta cell regeneration (Maningas *et al.*, 2013; Patra and Muthuraman, 2013; Sakthivel *et al.*, 2016; Sheeja *et al.*, 2016; Koneri *et al.,* 2018).

Kappaphycus alvarezii

Kappaphycus alvarezii (Brown algae) was investigated for anticonvulsant activity in mice by Yende *et al.* (2018). The anticonvulsant properties of marine algae were investigated in maximal electroshock-induced convulsion and Pentylenetetrazole (PTZ) - induced convulsion, and alkaloids, terpenoids, Flavonoids, steroids, and saponin were identified in the algae (Leila Hayashi and Renata Reis, 2012; Seetharaman *et al.*, 2016; Bhuyar *et al.*, 2020).

Gracilaria corticata

Gracilaria corticata are widely thought to be important because of their medicinal uses. Kain and Destombe (1995) investigated the bioactivities of the algae *Gracilaria corticata*, which is one of the most important species-rich in different elements responsible for a variety of pharmacological activities. *Gracilaria corticata* methanolic extracts are high in phenols and have a higher percentage of scavenging activity against nitric oxide, hydroxyl radicals, and hydrogen peroxide (Sampathkumar, 2008). *Gracilaria corticata* crude methanolic extracts were found to have significant antibacterial activity. It shows significant anticancer activity which was tested using different cancer cell lines like MCF7, normal Vero cell lines and Hep-G2 by MTT assay (Dist, 2013; Narasimhan *et al.*, 2013; Rout and Kumar, 2015).

Acanthophora specifera

Kumar and Jeyaprakash (2015) has reported in-vitro antioxidant efficacy and antimutagen on *Acanthophora specifera*. The study revealed the presence of saponin, tannin, Flavonoids, steroids, terpenoids, alkaloids, amino acids, polyphenol, anthraquinones, and glycosides. *In vitro* antioxidant property of *Acanthophora specifera* in respect to DPPH radical scavenging assay, Hydroxyl radical scavenging assay, Superoxide anion scavenging assay, nitric oxide scavenging assay, Fe^{2+} chelating assay, Reducing power assay and studied was suggested that the algae might have an antioxidant, anti-allergic, anti-inflammatory, anti-microbial, anti-cancer activity (Lavakumar and Ravichandiran, 2012; Shankhadarwar, 2015; Prasedya *et al.*, 2019).

Gelidiella acerosa

Syad *et al.* (2012) was assessed anticholinesterase (AChE), and butyryl-cholinesterase (BuChE) activities of *Gelidiella acerosa.* Benzene and ethyl acetate extract of *G. acerosa* showed positive results for the presence of terpenoids, cardiac glycosides, alkaloids, and tannins. GC-MS illustrates that the benzene extract possesses a high amount of terpenoids, which could be the reason for potential cholinesterase inhibitory activity (Blunden, 1993; Prasad *et al.*, 2007; Nobel Surya Pandidurai *et al.* (2014), Arif Nisha Syad *et al.* (2016); Nupur Sharma *et al.* (2017).

3. Conclusions

From the above review, we conclude that plants and algae have a very versatile lifestyle. Every part of the plants and algae is serving as a boon for all living ones all over the universe. Many medicinal plants and marine algae are studied for the treatment of many diseases of human beings along with animal diseases such as stomach pain, constipation, piles, dysentery, jaundice, diabetes, asthma, menstrual disorders, menstrual disorders, snake bite, skin diseases, etc.

4. References

1) Abou-Elela, Gehan M. Elnaby A.H., Hassan A.H. Ibrahim and Okbah M.A. (2009). Marine natural products and their potential applications as anti-infective agents. *World Appl Sci J.,* 7(7): 872–880.
2) Anon (2005). Seaweeds: Wonder Plants of the Sea. Aquaculture Foundation of India, Chennai, 30.
3) Araújo C.A.C., and Leon L.L. (2001). Biological Activities of Curcuma longa L. Mem Inst Oswaldo Cruz, Rio de Janeiro, 96(5): 723–728.
4) Arif Nisha Syad, Beema Shafreen Rajamohamed, Karutha Pandian Shunmugaiah and Pandima Devi Kasi (2016). Neuroprotective effect of the marine macroalga Gelidiella acerosa: identification of active compounds through bioactivity-guided fractionation. *Pharmaceutical Biology,* 54(10): 2073 – 2081.
5) Augusti K.T. (1996). Therapeutic values of onion (*Allium cepa* L.) and garlic (*Allium sativum* L.). *Indian J Exp Biol.,* 34: 634 - 640.
6) Bailey C. J., and Day C. (1989). Traditional plant medicine as treatments for diabetes. *Diabetes Care,* 12: 553 – 564.
7) Bamola N., Verma P., and Negi C. (2018). A Review on Some Traditional Medicinal Plants. *Int. J. Life. Sci. Scienti. Res.,* 4(1): 1550 – 1556.
8) Bhuyar P., Rahim M.H., Sundararaju S., Maniam G.P., and Govindan N. (2020). Antioxidant and antibacterial activity of red seaweed; *Kappaphycus*

alvarezii against pathogenic bacteria. *Global J. Environ. Sci. Manag.,* 6(1): 47 – 58.

9) Blunden G. (1993). Marine algae as sources of biologically active compounds. *Interdisciplinary Science Reviews,* 18: 73 – 80.

10) Chavan P. A. (2016). Evaluation of Antimicrobial activity of Various Medicinal Plants Extracts of Latur Zone against Pathogens. *Int. J. Life. Sci. Scienti. Res.,* 2(5): 612 – 618.

11) Dist A. (2013). Antioxidant and brine shrimp cytotoxic activities of ethanolic extract of Red alga *Gracilaria corticata*. *Indian J Nat Prod Resour.,* 4(2): 233 – 237.

12) El-Gamal A. A. (2010). Biological importance of marine algae. *Saudi Pharm J.,* 18: 1 – 25.

13) Goel A., Kunnumakkara A. B and Aggarwal B. B. (2008). Curcumin as "Curecumin": From kitchen to clinic. *Biochemical Pharmacology,* 75(4): 787 – 809.

14) Eidi A., Eidi M., and Esmaeili E. (2006). Antidiabetic effect of garlic (*Allium sativum* L.) in normal and Streptozotocin - induced diabetic rats. *Phytomedicine*, 13: 624 – 629.

15) Guillermo D., Villamil L., and Almanza V. (2007). Herbivory effects on the morphology of the brown alga *Padina boergesenii* (Phaeophyta). *Phycol.*, 46(2): 131 – 136.

16) Guven K.C., Percot A., and Sezik E. (2010). Alkaloids in marine algae. *Mar. Drugs,* 8: 269 – 284.

17) Hamman J.H. (2008). Composition and Applications of *Aloe vera* Leaf Gel. *Molecules*, 13: 1599 – 1616.

18) Harini K., and Nithyalakshmi V. (2017). Phytochemical Analysis and Antioxidant Potential of Cucumis Melo Seeds. *Int. J. Life. Sci. Scienti. Res.,* 3(1): 863 - 867.

19) Kain J. M and Destombe C. (1995). A review of the life history, reproduction and phenology of *Gracilaria*. *J Appl Phycol.,* 7: 269 – 281.

20) Koneri R., Jha D. K., and Mubasheera M. G. (2018). An investigation on the type I antidiabetic activity of methanolic extract of Marine algae, *Gracilaria edulis* and *Sargassum polycystum*. *Int J Pharm Sci Res.,* 9(7): 2952 – 2959.

21) Kumar R.R., and Jeyaprakash K. (2015). Screening of phytochemical and in-vitro antioxidant efficacy on selected red seaweed (*Acanthophora specifera*) collected from Gulf of Mannar, Tamil Nadu, India. *World Journal of Pharmaceutical Research,* 4(6): 1505 – 1518.

22) Lavakumar V., and Ravichandiran V. (2012). Antimicrobial activity of *Acanthophora spicifera*. *Int. J. Res. Pharm. Sci.,* 3(1): 176 – 178.

23) Leila Hayashi and Renata P. Reis (2012). Cultivation of the red algae *Kappaphycus alvarezii* in Brazil and its pharmacological potential. *Revista Brasileira de Farmacognosia*, 22(4): 115 - 120.
24) Li X., and Tian T. (2018). Phytochemical Characterization of Mentha spicata L. Under Differential Dried-Conditions and Associated Nephrotoxicity Screening of Main Compound with Organ-on-a-Chip. *Front. Pharmacol.,* 9: 1067.
25) Louay Labban (2014). Medicinal and pharmacological properties of Turmeric (*Curcuma longa*): A review. *Int J Pharm Biomed Sci.,* 5(1): 17 – 23.
26) Mahendra C. Gunde and Nikhil D. Amnerkar (2016). Nutritional, medicinal and pharmacological properties of papaya (*Carica papaya* Linn.): A review. *Journal of Innovations in Pharmaceuticals and Biological Sciences,* 3(1): 162 – 169.
27) Mahesh B., and Satish S. (2008). Antimicrobial activity of some important medicinal plant against plant and human pathogens. *World Journal of Applied Science*, 4: 839 – 843.
28) Maningas M.B.B., Gonzalez P.G., Obias M.M., Pausanos R.S., Siapno J.L.Y., Alambra J.R., and Abquina E.M. (2013). Immune response of *Macrobrachium rosenbergii* immersed in hot-water extract of *Gracilaria edulis. Philipp. Sci. Lett.,* 6: 147 – 152.
29) McHugh D. J. (2003). A guide to the seaweed industry. *FAO Fisheries Technical Paper*, 441: 105.
30) Mohammed A., Adelaiye A.B., Abubakar M.S. and Abdurahman E.M. (2007). Effects of aqueous extract of *Ganoderma lucidum* on blood glucose levels of normoglycemic and alloxan-induced diabetic Wistar rats. *J. Medicinal Plants Res.,* 1(2): 34 – 37.
31) Mohammed S. Ali-Shtayeh, Rana M. Jamous, Salam Y. Abu-Zaitoun, Ahmad I. Khasati, Samer R. Kalbouneh (2019). Biological Properties and Bioactive Components of Mentha spicata L. Essential Oil: Focus on Potential Benefits in the Treatment of Obesity, Alzheimer's Disease, Dermatophytosis, and Drug-Resistant Infections", Evidence-Based Complementary and Alternative Medicine, 11, https://doi.org/10.1155/2019/3834265
32) Muthuvelan B., Chennubhotla V.S.K., Nair K.V.K., Sampath V., and Ravindran M. (2001). Standing crop biomass and comparative distribution of agarophytes, alginophytes and other algae in South Andaman. *Indian Hydrobiol.,* 4: 130 – 138.
33) Narasimhan M. K., Pavithra S. K., Krishnana V., and Chandrasekaran M. (2013). *In vitro* analysis of antioxidant, antimicrobial and antiproliferative

activity of *Enteromorpha antenna, Enteromorpha linza* and *Gracilaria corticata* extracts. *Jundishapur J Nat Pharm Prod.,* 8(4): 151 – 159.

34) Narendiran S., Janani D., Keerthana M., Nivethitha K.S., Nirmala Devi S., Padmavathy S., Supraja T.S., Sayeedur Rahman H., Velvizhi R., Swathi N., and Yasaswini K.G. (2016). Comparative Studies on in-vitro Phytochemicals Analysis and Larvicidal Efficacy of Medicinal Plant Extracts against *Culex quinquefasciatus. Int. J. Life. Sci. Scienti. Res.,* 2(6): 742 – 748.

35) Nishant P. (2016). Role of Medicinal Plants (Brahmi and Ashwagandha) in the Treatment of Alzheimer's Disease. *Int. J. Life. Sci. Scienti. Res.,* 2(1): 15 – 17.

36) Nobel Surya Pandidurai R., Kalavathi K., and Perumal P. (2014). Studies on antibacterial activity of seaweeds, *Enteromorpha intestinalis* (Linnaeus) and *Gelidiella acerosa* (Forsskal) from Puducherry and Rameswaram (Southeast coast of India). *International Journal of Pharma and Bio Sciences,* 5(1): 1139 – 1147.

37) Nupur Sharma. (2017). *Gelidiella acerosa*: A Précis. *Int. Res. J. Pharm.*, 8(4): 20 – 23.

38) Nwosu F., Morris J., Victoria A.L., Stewart D., and Heather A. (2011). Anti-proliferative and potential anti-diabetic effects of phenolic-rich extracts from edible marine algae. *Food Chemistry,* 126: 1006 – 1012.

39) Pandit R., Phadke A., and Jagtap A. (2010). Antidiabetic effect of *Ficus religiosa* extract in Streptozotocin-induced diabetic rats. *J. Ethnopharmacol.,* 128: 462 – 466.

40) Patra S., and Muthuraman M.S. (2013). *Gracilaria edulis* extract induces apoptosis and inhibits tumor in *Ehrlich ascites* tumor cells *in vivo. BMC Complement. Altern. Med.,* 13: 331 - 340.

41) Prasad K., Siddhanta A.K., Ganesan M., Ramavat B.K., Jha B., Ghosh Pushpito K. (2007). Agars of *Gelidiella acerosa* of west and southeast coasts of India. *PubMed,* 98(10): 1907 – 1915.

42) Prasedya E.S., Martyasari N.W.R., Hamdin C.D., Miyake M., Kobayashi D., Widyastuti S., Hazama A., and Sunarpi H. (2019). Effectiveness of Methanol Solvent Extraction for Red Macroalgae *Acanthophora spicifera* Antitumor Activity. *Pharmacog J.,* 11(3): 450 – 454.

43) Priyadarshi A., and Ram B. (2018). A review on pharmacognosy, phytochemistry and pharmacological activity of *Carica papaya* (linn) leaf. *Int J Pharm Sci. Res.,* 9(10): 4071 – 4078.

44) Priyanka Sharma, Amit C. Kharkwal, Harsha Kharkwal, Abdin M.Z. and Ajit Varma (2014). A Review on Pharmacological Properties of *Aloe vera. Int. J. Pharm. Sci. Rev. Res.,* 29(2): 31 – 37.

45) Rajamani K., Manivasagam T., and Ananatharaman P. (2010). Chemopreventive effect of *Padina boergesenii* on ferric nitrilotriacetate (Fe-NTA) induced oxidative damage in Wistar rats. *J Appl Phycol.,* 257(2): 257 – 263.
46) Rajeswari R., Umadevi M., Sharmila Rahale C., Pushpa R., Selvavenkadesh S., Sampath Kumar K.P., Bhowmik D. (2012). *Aloe vera*: The Miracle Plant Its Medicinal and Traditional Uses in India. *Journal of Pharmacognosy and Phytochemistry*, 1(4): 118 – 124.
47) Rahul Kumar Verma, Preeti Kumari, Rohit Kumar Maurya, Vijay Kumar, RB Verma and Rahul Kumar Singh (2018). Medicinal properties of turmeric (*Curcuma longa* L.): A review. *International Journal of Chemical Studies*, 6(4): 1354 – 1357.
48) Ravindran V.S., Thangaradjou T., and Kannan L. (2004). Qualitative and quantitative distribution of seaweeds in the Great Nicobar Island. Seaweeds – 2004 – National Symposium and Exposition, Cochin, Abst., 27.
49) Rout S., and Kumar A (2015). A review on the potentiality of marine seaweeds. *World Journal of Pharmacy and Pharmaceutical Sciences,* 4(10): 458 – 476.
50) Sagadevan P., Selvakumar S and Raghunath M. (2019). Medicinal properties of *Carica papaya* Linn: Review. *Madridge J Nov Drug Res.,* 3(1):120 – 125.
51) Sakthivel R., Muniasamy S., Archunan G., Devi K.P. (2016). *Gracilaria edulis* exhibit an-tiproliferative activity against human lung adenocarcinoma cell line A549 without causing adverse toxic effect *in vitro* and *in vivo*. *Food Funct.,* 7: 1155 – 1165.
52) Sahoo D., Sahu N., and Sahoo D. (2003). A critical survey of seaweed biodiversity of Chilika Lake, India. *Algae*, 18: 1–12.
53) Sampathkumar P. (2008). Potential hepatoprotective effect of aqueous extract of *Gracilaria corticata* in AFB1 induced hepatotoxicity in Wister rats. *J Biol Sci.,* 8(8): 1352 – 1355.
54) Seetharaman S., Indra V., Selva Muthu B., Daisy A. and Geetha S. (2016). Phytochemical profiling and antibacterial potential of *Kappaphycus alvarezii* methanol extract against clinical isolated bacteria. *World Journal of Pharmacy and Pharmaceutical Sciences*, 5(6): 1328 – 1333.
55) Senthilkumar P., Sudha S., and Prakash S. (2014). Antidiabetic activity of aqueous extract of *Padina boergesenii* in Streptozotocin-induced diabetic rats. *Int J Pharm Pharm Sci.,* 6(5): 418 – 422.
56) Sevindik M (2018) Pharmacological Properties of *Mentha* Species. *J Tradit Med Clin Nature*, 7: 259.

www.ingramcontent.com/pod-product-compliance
Ingram Content Group UK Ltd.
Pitfield, Milton Keynes, MK11 3LW, UK
UKHW061550190726
13845UKWH00030B/1100

9 788195 132379